An Adoption Diary

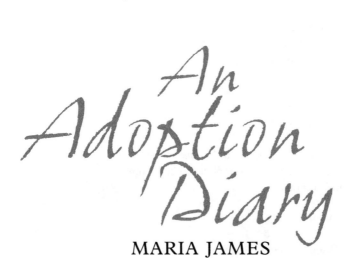

An Adoption Diary

MARIA JAMES

Published by
British Association for Adoption & Fostering
(BAAF)
Saffron House
6–10 Kirby Street
London EC1N 8TS
www.baaf.org.uk

Charity registration 275689
© Maria James 2006

British Library Cataloguing in Publication Data
A catalogue record for this book is available from
the British Library

ISBN 1 903699 21 5

Project management by Shaila Shah, BAAF
Photographs on cover posed by models
by John Birdsall Photography www.johnbirdsall.co.uk
and www.istockphoto.com
Designed by Andrew Haig & Associates
Typeset by Fravashi Aga
Printed in Great Britain by T J International

BAAF is the leading UK-wide membership organisation
for all those concerned with adoption, fostering and
child care issues.

Acknowledgements
I am grateful to my husband, Rob, for his love and
patience and for his computer skills, and to my mother
for her unfailing belief in me as a parent and as a writer.
I would like to thank Hedi Argent for her advice, support
and encouragement in producing this book, Audrey
Cornelius for commenting on an earlier draft, and
BAAF for publishing it.

Some names have been changed for the purpose
of publication in order to protect identity.

About the author
Maria James was born in Sussex in 1965. She is married
to Rob and they live in South East England with their son
and three dogs. This is her first book. She is currently
working on a novel.

The Our Story series
This book is the first in a new series to be published by
BAAF which will explore adoption experiences as told by
adoptive parents.

The series editor
Hedi Argent is the editor of this series. She is an
independent adoption consultant, trainer and freelance
writer. She is the author of *Find me a Family* (Souvenir
Press, 1984), *Whatever Happened to Adam?* (BAAF, 1998),
Related by Adoption (BAAF, 2004), *One of the Family*
(BAAF, 2005), the co-author of *Taking Extra Care*
(BAAF, 1997) and the editor of *Keeping the Doors Open*
(BAAF, 1988), *See you Soon* (BAAF, 1995), *Staying
Connected* (BAAF, 2002) and *Models of Adoption Support*
(BAAF, 2003). She has also contributed four illustrated
booklets to the children's series published by BAAF:
What Happens in Court? (2003), *What is Contact?* (2004),
What is a Disability? (2004) and *Life Story Work* (2005)
with Shaila Shah.

Contents

For our son

1

Back to the beginning

APRIL 2002

It's funny you know. I reckon just about every little girl imagines herself to be a mum one day; imagines herself being the sort of parent that children can only dream about.

You know – best friend and agony aunt rolled into one; the proud mother of the bride or groom; the doting grandmother who bakes the yummiest cakes and thinks the internet will never replace a good book. I'm sure the list goes on. Therefore you almost take it for granted that being a mum one day is a "rite of passage" – a part of settling down and creating your own "nest".

So it comes as a bit of a shock when, after years of trying for a baby, you eventually come to realise that it's never going to happen. Being a mum, that is. Being the one thing that you took for granted. If the career didn't take off, you knew that a mother's work was just as valuable – if not more so.

It is something that every woman should have the chance to experience, if she wants to. To feel a baby growing inside her. To give life to another human being.

It almost never occurs to you, you see, that you just might not be able to. That you might not be able to have

1

your partner's child. That your parents might never get to enjoy spoiling their grandchildren. That you might never get to be a grandparent yourself.

And, unless you're very careful when you think about those things, you can find yourself feeling guilty for not being able to conceive. You can even convince yourself that you're something of a failure. You're not normal – not a real woman. You're not like your best friend, or your sister or your sixteen-year-old neighbour. You won't be going to "mother & toddler" groups or school nativity plays; you won't ever experience that first tooth, that first step or the first time your child says 'why?'.

Nobody can fully understand how that makes a woman feel. Nobody, that is, except any other woman who has gone through, or is going through, exactly the same thing, and there are lots of us out there.

So, the big question is, what do you do about it when you finally realise that you can't have children? Apart from scream that is. And holler. And bawl your heart out to all and sundry. Then you might get bitter. You might have strong feelings of anger, self-pity and think, 'why me'? You will undoubtedly feel as if a knife has gone through you every time a friend or colleague tells you they are pregnant. I know I did.

I grew resentful of those women who could "fall" within the first month of trying. Those women who plan the second child according to the four seasons – 'I just couldn't go through another summer pregnancy!'

I'd avoid school reunions in case I was the only woman from my class who couldn't bear children. I'd resent the fact that sometimes people would assume that my husband and I didn't want a child – or even worse, tell me to my face, 'You shouldn't leave it too long Maria…what with your age and all'. I quickly came to the conclusion that people can be unbelievably insensitive.

But then there are those who feel every single bit of pain with you.

Family. Especially your mother. She, who has supported you through all your years of growing up and feels helpless as she watches and waits for a miracle to happen.

Friends suffer too. It breaks their hearts almost as much as it does your own. They dread telling you that they are trying for a baby. They dread even more telling you that they are pregnant. Obviously you are happy for them and genuinely share in their joy. Then you go back home and cry on your partner's shoulder – he who gets the brunt of the anguish time and time again. It's a long hard road, that's for sure, and yet somehow you do eventually have to find your way through.

Some people try IVF as a means to achieve their goal. There are several different techniques for In Vitro Fertilisation, but usually if a woman can't conceive, she will take fertility drugs to help her produce more eggs. These eggs are then harvested and fertilised in a laboratory. After taking further hormonal drugs, the fertilised eggs are placed in her womb – with the hope that a pregnancy will follow.

But sometimes, if the woman does not ovulate satisfactorily, another woman's eggs will need to be fertilised with her partner's sperm. This would have been our scenario – and the success rate is extremely low.

So although I sincerely understand that very real need to exhaust every possible option, Rob and I simply chose not to take this path. We knew that IVF failure puts a relationship to the test time and time again and costs a couple dearly in both emotional and financial terms. We knew that it was not for us.

Then, of course, there is always surrogacy, which I'm sure most involuntarily childless couples have talked about on at least one occasion. We certainly did – and maybe if surrogacy was as open an option here as it is in the United States, then we might have investigated a little further. I know that there are numerous success stories people can tell, but there are also a lot of risks involved. As we stand at present, there is no legally binding contract to ensure that at the very last minute the surrogate mum might not change her mind. Even if the whole process goes smoothly, there is still this very unfair stigma attached to surrogacy in this country. Hence some couples have tried to go abroad, facing citizenship problems for their child on their return. I believe that, in principle, surrogacy is one of the most selfless things that one woman can do for another. It's just that, once again, this was not the path that Rob and I wanted to take. Especially when there are so many children in care already – each and every one of them needing good and loving parents.

Which brings us back to the whole infertility issue again. Just how do you go about reconciling yourself to the fact that you will never know the joy of being a natural or biological mother? For me, having a faith helped a lot, though I'm not so naïve as to think that this would comfort everyone facing infertility. It just helped me get things in perspective, and I always felt that God had hidden plans up his sleeve – like adoption, for example.

This was something that we had talked about at length, putting it on the back burner until we felt brave enough to proceed further. For us, especially me, the whole process of adoption was just too scary and all the negative press over the years had only reinforced our preconceptions.

I mean, if you were overweight you could forget adoption, couldn't you?

If you smoked a little, drank a little – then surely you weren't suitable adopters.

What if you worked full-time? What if you kept dogs? Didn't you have to be virtually perfect to adopt in this country – and didn't the process take many years?

Yes – maybe a lot of that was true once. It was off-putting for many people, who, like us, felt that the judging would be too much to bear. The image of the social worker playing God was one that I personally felt I didn't know if I could handle. However, as the end result was one that we both so much wanted, we felt we just had to give it a try. It was at that moment also, that I decided to write a book about the whole process – from the very beginning to the final court date, when a child might legally become ours.

I imagined the book to be a diary – a personal account that we could present to you, our adopted child-to-be, as a loving keepsake, so that you might "share" our journey although you could not be with us from the beginning. I also reckoned such a book would have been extremely helpful for Robbie and me when we first started the adoption process. I hoped that a diary might enlighten others who were in the throes of thinking about adoption.

So where, exactly, do you start when you are thinking about adopting a child? The local social services department (now Children's Services) is an obvious choice for many people. We lived in the southeast of England, so we contacted our local borough council as our first port of call. Although the adoption department was interested in our enquiry, there was to be a wait of many months before a member of the team could even come and talk to us about what was involved. This, I'm led to believe, is quite normal; departments are often under-funded and under-staffed. It made us decide to broaden our search to further afield.

We had already subscribed to an excellent publication called *Be My Parent*, which features children waiting for adoption and also has bi-monthly articles of interest. We'd found the publication on the Internet, on the BAAF website (British Association for Adoption & Fostering). BAAF also sent us a list of adoption agencies, both local authority and voluntary, to whom we could apply to adopt a child.

I think that in the end we looked at five agencies, as well as our own local social services department.

Each agency sent us detailed information regarding the whole process of adoption: the criteria for adopters, the sort of children who needed parents, and the emotional

5

implications of placing a child with a new family. Each agency seemed to have its own particular procedures but they more or less followed the same pattern.

The first step was filling in a preliminary application form, stating what age child we would be looking to adopt, whether we preferred a girl or a boy, and also providing basic information about ourselves. More difficult to fill in were a series of boxes regarding children who might be placed for adoption. Could we be loving and committed parents to, say, a child with developmental problems? Or a child who had been physically or sexually abused? Or a child with a history of severe mental illness in the family? Or a child who may need lifetime medical treatment or special education? These were all factors requiring deep discussion, and Robbie and I spent a long time thinking about each and every category.

Some of the agencies hold a sort of "open evening" discussion group, giving out lots of information and then, at the end of the evening, if people are still interested, they can make an initial application and proceed. The agency which Rob and I were interested in did not operate like that. They sent us information and the form to fill in and explained that, if they felt they could take up our application, they would write to us and ask us to attend an interview at their agency.

So that is what they did – and very promptly too.

Thursday 4 April 2002
The agency we have chosen is a voluntary agency in South London. We are only just within its fifty-mile radius but it is one we instantly felt comfortable with. They are also open to working hand in hand with the *Be My Parent* publication and Adoption UK, another excellent organisation, run by adopters for adopters. More importantly, the agency is looking to place the sort of children we feel we could give a strong and loving home to. They are always ready and willing to answer any questions

over the telephone – and they always return my calls as soon as they can.

This, I must point out, is not always the case with other adoption agencies, in fact one agency never got back to us at all.

So all in all, Rob and I are really looking forward to this first "official" discussion about the possibility of adoption. We don't quite know what to expect – whether it will be a startlingly formal meeting with a panel of stern-faced social workers, or an informal chat with someone we like!

In the event, it turns out to be the latter.

We arrive at the agency, both of us incredibly nervous. I am more unsteady than Rob, managing to imagine the very worst of scenarios. However, all such fears and worries are soon dispelled when a warm, informally dressed social worker greets us with a firm handshake. We immediately relax. Led to a room and plied with cups of tea, we begin our discussion, which lasts about an hour and a half.

It is good, I have to say. At no time are we made to feel that we have to be perfect in order to offer a home to a child. At no time do we feel that we have to watch what we are saying in case we say the wrong thing. Some of what the social worker tells us is positively uplifting. Having been told by many agencies that I am too old to be considered for a baby (I'm approaching my thirty-seventh birthday), it is refreshing to be told that we are among the younger adopters to apply. Rob is eight years younger than me – it's true – but it's not as if I am ready to collect my bus pass or incapable of running around with a lively toddler!

No, this particular agency does not have a problem with age or the fact that we have dogs, one of them a large, but soppy, deerhound.

We are asked about our lifestyle and our families. We explain that we live in a small town in the country, close to the seaside and yet only an hour away from London. Our families live nearby and are frequent visitors to our home, which is three-bedroomed, smart and detached. I have a love for writing, as well as working voluntarily with the blind. Rob is a brilliant computer analyst. We have a wonderful eclectic mix of friends, all living within a thirty-mile radius, some with children, some without. Our dogs are our passion (we have two) – as well as music, books, food and travelling to Europe. We're not poor, we're not rich, but we're happy with what we have and long to share it with our child.

We are asked about the sort of children we feel we could offer a good home to and the sort of children that we would not be able to cope with. For us, this includes children with severe disabilities, such as cerebral palsy, and also children whose parents have a history of serious mental illness. We are open to discussing letterbox and direct contact with birth families (something all agencies advocate is in the best interest of the child nowadays), and we talk about the obvious and hidden impact of neglect and abuse and the subsequent effects on a child. The only time in the whole conversation that the social worker draws a sharp breath is when I tell her that I smoke.

This is like saying I had butchered my grandmother with a carving knife. Well, not quite, but it is something that is extremely frowned upon, and is continually commented on throughout the process, even though I only smoke one packet a week.

At least I feel I've been honest. In retrospect, it would have been easier to lie. I can only presume that those people who own up to smoking heavily would never get a look in, which is quite harsh.

Back to the interview, and our social worker simply asks me whether I want to give up, to which I obviously say, 'yes'. She doesn't labour the subject too much after that, although the guilt I feel for my confessed "sin" is immense.

After ninety minutes we have explored the kind of child, and the age, we might be suitable adopters for. Nothing definite, just a preliminary chat. The social worker mentions a few times that she is not here to discourage us and says – quote – 'we need people like you'. All in all it has been a very fair exchange.

We initially put age three – five as a guideline for the age of child we were hoping to adopt. After our discussion the social worker thinks that we could aim for younger than that, and she writes 0 – 5 on the form, although, she says, a child over the age of two is going to be more appropriate with us having a large dog in the house – and also because I smoke. As a rule of thumb they do not like to place a child under the age of two with a smoker. Fair enough. We are just more than happy that we will be considered for a child aged two – five. Some agencies are only looking for suitable adopters for children of school age and over. It would be lovely to give a home to any child – but it would be even lovelier to be able to form a bond with a child who was that much younger.

We have also been asked if we will consider adopting siblings – brothers and sisters together. We say 'no'. Another adoption in the future is not out of the question, but we feel more comfortable with initially having one child to whom we can give our undivided attention.

So that is that, really. Rob and I stress that we are open to adopting a boy or a girl – on the basis that if we had managed to conceive naturally we would have been thrilled with either.

The social worker seems pleased with how things have gone. She mutters something about it 'all looking very good to me' but then explains that the notes she has been making will have to be presented as a report to the next team meeting of social workers at the agency, to be held on 16 April. At that stage they will decide whether to proceed with us. They will write to us with their decision, enclosing a formal application form if the answer is positive. The next step, as with most agencies, would be for both Rob and me to attend a series of preparation workshops on adoption. Then there would be a medical with our local doctor. There would be a police check and three references from two friends and a family member (two of whom would be visited). Then there would be the infamous "home study" or assessment, which would take approximately six months. Then the moment we would be waiting for – an adoption panel would decide whether to recommend that we be approved as adopters or not.

The excitement I feel is almost tangible. This may alter as time goes on! To sit discussing children and adoption with a social worker somehow makes it seem possible. What we had planned for so many years now seems like it can become a reality.

Thursday 18 April 2002
When a letter arrives on 18 April, I can hardly open the envelope quickly enough. The agency wishes to pursue our enquiry and, furthermore, we are being invited to the May 2002 set of preparation workshops.

Almost incredulous, we realise that the first day of the workshop is therefore less than one month away. Our family and friends are ecstatic at the news, but everyone, not least of all us, assumes that the whole process is going to take a very long time.

We fill in the application form, attach recent photos of ourselves, and give two of our closest friends as referees, and my mother as the third. I feel it is important to include my mum in the process somehow, for without her encouragement I sometimes wonder whether I would have reached this stage – my self-esteem having taken quite a few knocks over the past eight years.

The next step on the agenda is for Rob and me to provide doctors' details and for each of us to fill in a police check form. These will not be processed until after we have attended the preparation workshops in case, I suppose, we decide to have a break from proceedings or choose not to continue at all.

Finally, all Robbie and I have to do is wait, until Saturday 11 May to be precise, for the first of our four preparation workshops. Both of us are nervous and unsure of exactly what to expect. We try to get on with our lives in as normal a fashion as possible (which is what everyone tells you to do), and before we know it, the day is actually upon us. It has come round almost frighteningly quickly. Somehow the dream of becoming a parent is that little bit closer.

2

Our first adoption workshops

MAY 2002

I've never really relished "Induction" days whenever I've started a new job. The "Introductions" in particular terrify me – standing up, apprehensive, red-faced, struggling to describe my finer points for the delight of a captive audience.

I wonder what I might say about myself, if asked, at our first adoption workshop. I imagine I would say that I'm gregarious, caring, a good friend, an avid reader, a dog lover, knowledgeable about wine, an aspiring novelist and a dreadful cook.

If asked about my husband, I would say that he is witty, dependable, a good listener, a Mini (car) fanatic, hideously untidy, brilliant with computers – and my very best friend.

So I start to wonder, as the day of reckoning beckons, will we actually have to stand and announce ourselves or will I be able to remain anonymous – a vigilant observer, quietly blending into the background?

Saturday 11 May 2002
When it comes, the morning could not have had a more

disastrous start. Just as we are about to head for the train station, en-route to London, we have an electrical fire in the hallway. Clearly not wanting to leave an unsafe house, we have to leave a message for our adoption agency and hastily call out an electrician.

This does nothing to help our nerves. It is the first day of our adoption workshop and all is not well!

Ringing our agency once more, I explain that with two train connections to catch, we will be with them by 11am. The course is due to start at 9.45am. We will be at an instant disadvantage and will feel decidedly uncomfortable walking in on a room full of people, probably all staring at us. What a great start to the day. We assure each other that the reality cannot be that bad.

But it is.

It is awful.

Sixteen people, all wearing name badges, sitting in a grim-faced circle. If it hadn't been for the amiable social worker, trying to make us feel welcome, I think we'd have walked out then and there. I console myself that at least we have missed the introductions.

Everyone breaks for coffee after we arrive, so this gives the social worker time to fill us in on what we have missed. Then our name badges and folder of notes are handed to us, and we take our seats in the circle. I immediately feel sick with nerves.

The first exercise after the break is "ripping paper". It is powerful stuff and a very clever way of bringing home the upheaval that most adopted children have suffered in their short lives. The social worker, Dee, takes a large sheet of paper and asks us all to contribute experiences and factors that make us the person we are today. She writes down: home, parents, school, friends, pets, hobbies, travel, stability, family, guidance, discipline, neighbours, clubs, holidays. These are just a few of the suggestions put forward. Dee then takes the large sheet of paper and rips it into shreds, symbolic of the fragmented life of the adopted child.

Quite thought-provoking really, like literally having the rug pulled from beneath your feet. Every facet of the child's life, any pattern of continuity just torn to pieces as the child is moved time and time again – saying goodbye to parents, siblings, carers, peers and a house they probably thought was their home.

Dee then scatters the torn pieces of paper onto the floor in a complete jumble; a few pieces flutter away and are lost altogether. She demonstrates just how difficult it is to try and put the bits back together again, like a jigsaw with missing pieces. Most of them just do not seem to fit and it would take masses of patience and time to fit them together again properly.

In much the same way as an adopted child would probably come to us with his or her entire history scattered in tiny pieces.

The next exercise is equally powerful and beautifully simple. A second social worker shows us a bag containing a few treasured possessions, which a six-year-old may have accumulated over the years – maybe it's a faded scarf or a Christmas card from a foster carer, an old train ticket, a broken toy, or something that reminds them of a sister or brother. There is no need for words. The exercise serves to reinforce what should have been obvious to us: that all of the child's belongings should be kept in a special, safe place, not washed and tidied away, and that children should be encouraged to talk about the contents of their treasure bag or box whenever they want to.

It is a very moving exercise and many people begin to look visibly upset.

It is surprising to see that there isn't a broader cross-section of people on our course. We expected more single applicants, more council tenants and not just "home-owners". They pretty much all live in London apart from Rob and me – and quite a few of them already have children, which is another surprise to us. A lot of them are quite a bit older than we are – perhaps a factor in how solvent they appear to be, which one couple seems at pains to emphasise. They point out that, although they have a huge house, their own businesses and lots of money, they still feel excluded from their neighbours' gatherings because they don't have children. It is as if money can buy them everything else in life and yet they still don't fit in – so enter the adopted child to help ease matters at their next summer barbecue.

It is astounding to hear this particular couple's motivation for adoption. Nearly everyone else on our course seems very pleasant and as nervous as we are. It is just not quite what we'd been expecting.

On a more positive note, however, it is encouraging to see three couples of mixed ethnicity and an Asian couple on our course, as it is common knowledge that there are not enough black or mixed ethnicity adopters coming forward. Often black children and children of dual heritage end up staying in care for a very long time, so it is great to see that we are not all white.

Group work comes next. It is one of the things that I've been dreading most – often lacking in confidence in such situations.

It just shows how wrong you can be.

This first group-work exercise, in fact, is a turning point for us all – enabling everyone to interact with one another and certainly helping us all to relax a bit more. We work together on the "Adoption Triangle". Basically, it involves looking at the adoption process from the child's, birth family's and the adopters' point of view.

We have to chart both the losses and the gains of an adoption, and in my group we have to work from the child's perspective. It is terribly easy to list the losses a child has suffered. Fortunately we can think of many gains too: a loving family and stable home, security, safety, the opportunity to express themselves honestly, perhaps the chance to bond with a new brother or sister or a pet. It is all very informative stuff.

Separated from me, Rob and his group have the more difficult task of seeing the adoption from the birth family's point of view. My initial thoughts on this had been fairly black and white. If the child was given up for adoption or taken into care because the parents could not bring up their children, or neglected or ill-treated them in any way, then I reckoned that was their look out – and they should deal with the consequences accordingly.

I'd never before looked at the middle ground – the grey area in between. The exercise shows me that the emotional impact on the whole birth family is immense – we're not just talking about the birth parents here.

What about the grandparents?

What about the siblings?

The impact of an adoption is obviously felt by a wide circle of people. It also teaches me that for a mother to give up a child, or have a child taken into care, is never a cut and dried situation, never a final ending. It opens my eyes to the pain that is involved, and rather than feeling quite indifferent to the birth family's anguish, I now feel a strong degree of empathy in many of the cases.

The third group completes the adoption triangle by discussing things from the adopters' perspective. They particularly address contact with the birth family and the importance of letterbox contact, seen as essential so that an adopted child does not feel abandoned or forgotten by their birth family.

However, the best bit of this first workshop for most people is, without doubt, the adopters' talk. A couple who have adopted two young children through the agency have come to tell us of their experiences and to remind us that they once sat where we are now – feeling just as overwhelmed and apprehensive.

It is a wonderfully positive message to us all – and a much needed lift to the spirits. Two points especially make their mark on Rob and me.

Firstly, just how many times these young children have

been moved from home to home. A two-year-old may have moved house twenty times or more. Unthinkable, isn't it? I mean, as an adult how stressful do we find one house move? Bear in mind that at least for us that usually means moving with the same people – staying with the people we love, our family.

Not so for the adopted child.

So a poignant comment comes from the father of the adopted children. It had taken his little girl almost a year to learn to trust and bond with him – never having had a positive male role model in her life before.

Secondly, it took many months for that same little girl to believe that she wasn't going to be moved on again and that yet another family had not given up on her. She used to ask visiting family and friends if they were going to be her new mummy and daddy. The concept of a permanent, stable home was not one she had encountered. Over time, this little girl began to understand that this mummy and daddy would love her for life. She was not going to be moved any more.

It is a very touching moment for me and brings home the sheer emotional insecurity that these children must feel before eventually learning to accept love in a permanent adoptive home.

So we leave, armed with reading material and homework, which is answering a questionnaire on "separation and loss" and the probable effect on a child when removed from their birth family. The workshop has been intense and everyone by now is mentally exhausted and in need of fresh air.

It has been a lot to take on board for the first day of a workshop – and all I can think of is that we have another three days to go!

Thursday 16 May 2002
If we thought the first day of the workshop had dealt with painful issues, then we were in for something of a shock on

day number two.

The social workers, different today, but just as pleasant, warn us that the morning will deal with some very heavy issues, such as attachment disorder, separation and loss and child abuse – particularly sexual abuse.

They are not wrong. No wonder one of them fears that we won't come back after lunch!

After briefly discussing child development, it is the terrible seriousness of attachment disorder that makes me realise why some people choose to drop out of the course. Nobody is opting out of our course yet, so we are obviously made of stronger stuff!

The social worker emphasises that not all children suffer from this condition and, in fact, some doctors still dispute the actual existence of attachment disorder. But it appears to be a very understandable reaction to years of neglect, moves in and out of care, and never having the chance to form nurturing bonds with a parent figure. Basic stuff even, like the eye contact when babies feed.

What can then happen is that the child fails to respond to love and affection when finally adopted. Children like that can be destructive, self-harming, constantly pushing against boundaries and incapable of understanding and giving love or warmth, so that placements can break down. Approximately one-tenth of the children placed by our agency in the last year showed varying degrees of attachment disorder. Other possible effects of poor early attachment experiences are severe temper tantrums, stealing, incessant questioning, learning problems and eating disorders. It is distressing to hear.

I have to be honest here. Although the social worker tries her very best to remain upbeat about the amount of professional help that is available if such problems arise, the whole subject matter is intensely depressing. To follow this discussion with one on separation and loss – and then another on sexual abuse – does seem too much in one go.

I'm not saying I'm averse to looking at these problems

head on – for if I was, then I shouldn't really be considering adoption. I do wonder, however, if we really have to concentrate on three such major issues all together. It is very intense.

The adopter's talk of the previous session seems far removed from today's themes. I think we could all have done with some sort of positive reminder of the joys that can also be experienced through adoption as well as the lows.

Separation and loss are the topics of our next group exercise. We have to discuss a child's poor self-image and how it would make us feel, and how we could try to improve the situation. We also have to consider how children seek attention through negative behaviour.

The discussion bonds us together. Everyone is much friendlier and a little more relaxed in this second session, and everyone's ideas are fascinating, especially those from people who have already raised children.

Sexual abuse is a subject that I think the majority of the people on the course feel uneasy talking about. The social worker – again excellent – seems more than aware of this and assures us that we will not do group exercises on such a personal and intimate matter.

The term "sexual abuse" is clarified for us – it can be physical contact or exposure to inappropriate videos and magazines as well as witnessing sexual behaviour first-hand. The result is that often children become very sexually aware. They might make explicit sexualised overtures, especially to adults. They may fear going to bed. They may obsessively wash and clean themselves. They may bed-wet and soil themselves. They may become suicidal as adults. It is hard stuff to take in.

Lunch is therefore a much-needed respite for us all. Everyone tends to disperse quickly, very few opting to join up with any others. All I feel like doing is walking quietly with Rob, neither of us having the need to talk.

Back to the workshop in the afternoon, and a different

social worker has come in to tell us about the legal terms used in adoption. This is an interesting talk, though quite a lot of information to remember straight off.

We discuss, amongst other things, parental responsibility, the Children Act, care orders and children freed for adoption. "Looked after children" is a new term for us, which apparently social workers have to use instead of "children in care". Also, one extra bit of information that I didn't know before, is that there are hardly any "children's homes" anymore – nearly all of the children who are placed for adoption will have come from foster homes.

The last part of the day is spent looking at a case study of a one-year-old boy who was moved from pillar to post because of constantly changing circumstances in his home life. We all have to play at being social workers, contributing as a group, and trying to make the right decisions as to where little Liam will reside. It really makes us see things from the social worker's point of view for a change, and we quickly realise how difficult it can be to get things right every time. For example, if the birth mother comes back, having apparently sorted out her problems, shouldn't she be entitled to another chance at bringing up her child? Absolutely yes; government policy is that, wherever possible, the child should remain with their birth family.

But what if the problems re-occur, and the child has to be placed in a foster home once more? And what if mum comes back another six months down the line, new permanent boyfriend in tow, life looking brighter in every way. What then? Does she deserve yet another chance? What if the birth father then rears his head and decides he wants custody? What if, after four or five more moves for Liam (mum and dad by now both changing their minds again and opting not to keep him), what if Grandma suddenly stakes her claim? What then?

The exercise clearly illustrates that the social worker's load is not a light one. We know only too well how quick the media are to pounce when they get it wrong – and yet just this one "game" shows how incredibly difficult it can be to get it right.

The consequences? Little Liam was finally prepared for an adoption placement at the grand old age of four-and-a-half – three years and six months after first being taken from his mother. Behavioural problems by that time included aggressive temper tantrums, bedwetting, failure to mix well with other children and inappropriate sexual behaviour. Such unbelievable damage at such a tender age. The impact of constantly moving from one home to another – all bonds repeatedly broken – was clear to see.

So that, in basic terms, was day two of our preparation workshops. With yet more homework, this time an extensive questionnaire on behaviour associated with "attachment disorder" and how we would deal with the hurt and anger of a traumatised child – a child who may find it impossible to bond with new parents. Rob and I feel weighed down by the day's subject matter and unable to switch off and chat about anything else.

It has been an exhausting but ultimately informative and rewarding day.

I can't, in all truthfulness, say that I have enjoyed it – but I can say that the amount of work the social workers put into it has been impressive. Certain issues have to be looked at, regardless of how distressing they might be. Each and every one of us undoubtedly has come away from the workshop having learnt a massive amount about the reality of adopting a child.

We have also learnt a lot towards turning that child's life around for the better – and that is a really positive message on which to end our second day.

3

Reality dawns

MAY–JUNE 2002

Thursday 23 May 2002

Disaster strikes as I am kept awake all night by the most appalling toothache and have to get an emergency appointment in the morning. Living so far away from our adoption agency, it is plain that I won't be able to attend day three of our preparation workshops. Rob – it seems – will have to go on his own. It will be interesting to go through the day together later on, to see how much my husband has learnt – and can teach me.

When Rob returns home in the early evening, he is tired but full of enthusiasm for the day. Apparently, the morning began with a talk from a visiting doctor who works very closely with the agency. Primarily, she explained a wide range of medical conditions of which we should be aware. She pointed out the particular questions one should ask about a child's family history, for example, knowing whether a child is premature and what sort of ante-natal care was provided, if any.

She described the multitude of problems caused by foetal alcohol syndrome – where the mother has drunk to excess during her pregnancy. Addiction to drugs and nicotine and the possible results of dependency were also addressed. Foetal alcohol syndrome is a very serious condition and one that I knew little about. It often results in very underweight babies who may experience learning difficulties or even suffer from cardiac defects, or facial deformities. Although babies of IV drug abusers may have withdrawal symptoms at birth and require treatment, they do not generally have specific physical or mental problems, although nothing is ever certain and problems could arise later.

The doctor then talked about various mental health problems, such as schizophrenia in birth parents as well as autism, manic depression and the risks of Hepatitis B or C. It seems that if both birth parents suffer from schizophrenia then a birth child will have a 45 per cent chance of inheriting the disorder. Bi-polar effective disorder – manic depression to you and me – may or may not be inherited, more often than not skipping a generation. Both are serious mental illnesses and adopters should think long and hard about whether they are prepared to take on a child who may develop the same problems as their birth parents, in later life.

Rob certainly conveys that he thinks the doctor's talk – and the additional reading material – have been both interesting and informative, looking at issues which most people on the workshop probably knew very little about.

After the talk there were two exercises, providing the basis for group discussions. The first involved looking at healthy and unhealthy boundaries. Everyone had a particular "instance" on a card and had to say whether they would consider it as healthy or unhealthy behaviour. "Instances" included a father explaining to his son how to put on a condom – is this a healthy lesson in growing up? Or is a father washing inside the vagina of his three-year-old daughter when bathing her, crossing an unhealthy boundary?

Although an interesting (but embarrassing) exercise, Rob said that for him a lot of the answers were often pure common sense and the healthy or unhealthy boundaries were patently obvious.

He found the second group exercise altogether more useful – looking at children's behaviours, especially inappropriate behaviour. Each group had to look at various behavioural patterns in children and work out how one would go about dealing with the problems. For example, control issues could be a common difficulty, manifesting itself in eating problems such as constantly refusing food or leaving large amounts on the plate. If children feel they have little or no control over any other areas of their life, they may try to exercise control over the one thing they feel they can – food.

Ways of easing the problem may include allowing the child to have a wider choice in more areas of their life – as well as about the food they eat.

Other behavioural problems discussed were stealing, scratching and picking at their own skin (suppressed anxiety and worries), telling lies and head banging – a very real sign of frustration. Listening to the child, empathising and distracting could all help, as well as seeking professional advice if the problems persist.

Rob brought home a video for me to watch, which is about a very disruptive five-year-old boy (he had already been excluded from two schools), and how he is helped to change his behaviour. Praising the boy for even the most insignificant thing seemed to have a remarkable effect on his self-esteem and consequent behaviour. Indeed, the video seemed to be as much about educating his parents in how to interact with their son, as it did about setting consistent boundaries in their everyday life. Watching the father (clearly depressed since losing his job) encourage his son when playing was a really moving moment. Rather than lashing out aggressively, the child responded with an impromptu hug.

The video shows that there is help out there if you need it – and it also shows that the help available could make a huge difference. Interestingly enough, the little boy on the video was not adopted, which clearly illustrates the point that any set of parents can encounter difficulties when bringing up a child, not just adoptive parents. Although I'd missed the workshop, Rob managed to relay a vast amount of information from the day. It made me look forward to our fourth and last instalment.

Saturday 25 May 2002
So, mishaps withstanding, it is the final day of our preparation workshop. On arrival I immediately sense that the mood and tone of the day are much more easygoing, even quite light-hearted at times.

Of the four days I find it the most enjoyable – probably because we do not concentrate on the negative aspects of adoption and also because the group as a whole interacts easily and with confidence, myself included.

We are introduced to two more social workers, each with a very different style to those met previously on the course. We begin by touching on the subject of discipline, smacking in particular rearing its ugly head.

Smacking should be avoided at all times. A smack to an abused child will mean something very different from what it will mean to a child who has otherwise not been ill-treated. If adoptive parents repeatedly choose to smack their children, then the child protection people will soon be knocking on their door asking all sorts of questions – not for a one-off incident or a "tap" on the hand but definitely if smacking is used as the main form of discipline in the home.

We then move on to the first main exercise of the day entitled "Life Story Work". This involves making up a book (like a baby book, but more detailed) with information, family photos, birthday cards, school reports, and letters, which tell the story of the child's past; to be continued after the move to new adoptive parents, so that the child has a full sense of his or her own history and roots.

We immediately separate into three groups and each one has a different child's history to illustrate. My group chooses to represent a little girl's life as a journey down a long winding road. We include such things as a birth certificate, photos of birth mum and dad, photos of first home and pets, photos of subsequent foster homes and foster carers. We also put in a McDonalds' straw from when her birth mother took her out for a meal on her fifth birthday.

The two other groups display the child's life more in book form with, for example, hand drawn pictures of their imaginary friends, favourite people and siblings they have left behind.

It is a thought-provoking exercise that amply illustrates the upheavals these children have endured. It shows how important it is to record all the good – and not so good – moments in their short lives. We wonder about the history of our child-to-be. We think it will be good to go on with the life story together when "you", still unknown to us, come to live with us in our home.

Telling your child that they are adopted is next on the agenda and, without a doubt, honesty has to be the best policy every time. A child growing up knowing that they are adopted will cope much better than, say, a teenager having the news sprung upon them on their sixteenth birthday. One of our friends, having been adopted at a very young age, constantly makes this point.

If ever there was an example of an adoption working beautifully, then it has to be hers. Her parents brought her up knowing that she was adopted and making her feel special and "chosen". I think this made her feel rather unique at school and it was something she grew up accepting and celebrating. She thinks that her parents handled the situation exactly as she would have chosen to herself. If they had not told her until she was older, it would have become an issue, and she would have resented her parents enormously for letting her "live a lie".

Obviously the circumstances of the adoption have to be handled with sensitivity and a great deal of thought. If the child is the product of rape or incest, then clearly this is not the sort of information you would blurt out to a five-year-old. Our social worker explains that this would probably have to be handled with professional help and counselling, and the impact on the child would have to be monitored closely.

Then we discuss the question of who has the right to know about a child's adoption and a child's past. For instance, a doctor and a teacher should certainly have at least some of this information, but older children may not appreciate everyone from the postman to the local butcher knowing every detail about their life. I mean, would I like it? I think not.

The very controversial issue of "continuing contact with the birth family" comes next – a subject that pretty much divides the group. Some people would prefer no contact at all, whilst others are more open to once or twice yearly meetings or letterbox contact.

The social worker points out that it is in our own best interests to be as honest as possible. What we feel about it will be taken into account when a child is eventually placed with us. Quite a lot of the couples – Rob and I included – feel more comfortable with face-to-face contact with siblings than with birth parents. We would welcome letterbox contact with the birth mother or father, as it might enable a child to ask questions and to have some sense of continuity. Direct contact, we fear, might prove too disruptive and unsettling. However, every adoption is different and a great deal would depend on the individual circumstances of the child. For example, if a child has been physically or sexually abused by the birth parents, there would probably be no contact at all with them. The question would then remain, whether the child would have direct contact with his or her siblings, or perhaps just letterbox contact once or twice a year.

I think that contact with siblings – in any shape or form – should not be discouraged if that is what a child wants. Having lost or given up so much in their lives, it seems very cruel to stop them keeping in touch with their own brothers and sisters. Ultimately, I think contact decisions should have a lot of input from the child. It is impossible to totally rule out anything until the facts, as well as the wishes and feelings in each case are known.

One other important question raised is whether we, as adoptive parents, would be willing to have a one-off meeting with the birth parents prior to the adoption. Apparently three-quarters of people who are given the chance take this opportunity to ask questions about the child and to get a first-hand impression of the parents, which children might want to know about at a later stage. Rob and I haven't come to any hard and fast decisions on this subject – so much would depend on the reasons why the child had been put up for adoption in the first place.

The last exercise of the day is called "trading places" – and this one is fun. It involves looking at the way society perceives people, often forming opinions about them based on nothing more than preconceived ideas. Groups are randomly selected, with a mix of both men and women. There are four groups in all and some of these groups are then sub-divided. The men in our group have to look at the way that women are stereotypically portrayed in society – you know, hopeless at map reading, best at housework – that sort of thing. They discuss the positive and negative things about being a woman and they discuss the more serious issues of inequality in the workplace and lack of personal safety. The pressure to conform to a certain "look" (size 10, perfect skin?) is also explored. Interestingly enough, the women in our group do not have to look at how men are stereotypically portrayed in society: an example of inequality perhaps?

Our group has to look at how adopted people are regarded in society today, the notion being that a person might be disadvantaged in some way by the "poor you" syndrome. Another group has to look at how gay people are treated by society, and the preconceived ideas about gay men in particular.

Although I believe that people's opinions are changing all the time, I still think that better education in schools, for pupils and teachers alike, would allow adopted children to integrate more easily and would help alleviate the chances of being bullied. This is one of the things that we look at: how being "different" could lead to being bullied at school or in the workplace.

We draw up an extensive list of factors that could set a person apart from other people. The list is really quite exhaustive, ranging from skin colour and sexuality, to accent, background or disability of some kind. Being adopted is just one of many "differences" in society today. I have to say that most of the adopted people I have known have not suffered any more – or any less – bullying than I did at school. And mine was just because I had red hair and was deemed a "swot"!

I think that as long as the adopted child is not treated as a victim or as a casualty of a poor start in life, then things are heading in the right direction. The positive aspects of adoption should be reinforced by legislation, the media and also at school, so that all children have a better understanding of what adoption means.

This last exercise is a good way to round off the four days of workshops. As enjoyable and informative as these days have been, they have also been emotionally exhausting and immensely hard work – so it is something of a relief that they have drawn to a close.

Our social worker ends the day by telling us all about what to expect next. She talks us through the next six months of home assessment, after which our Form F (the report of the home study and now called the Prospective

Adopter's Report) will go before an adoption panel for a recommendation for approval.

We must now complete our evaluation report of the adoption preparation groups – filling in what we have learned, how useful we have found it, and how well, we think, it had been presented. This will make up part of the preparation section of our Form F report. The evaluation has to be returned to the agency as soon as possible, so that a social worker can be allocated to begin the home study period of the assessment. Now our formal application form (returned some weeks earlier) will be processed and we will be sent the relevant information for police checks and medical examinations.

All of our homework has to be finished and be up-to-date before the home assessment can begin, as this will be discussed as part of the whole process.

At this point in the proceedings it seems as good a time as any to take a break. The next part of the adoption process will be crucial, and neither Robbie nor I want to disrupt the home study by taking a holiday half way through. So we have decided to head abroad now.

Wednesday 5 June 2002

At the unearthly hour of six in the morning we arrive at Gatwick airport, ready to catch our flight to Verona. Once we arrive in Italy we continue our journey by coach – taking in spectacular mountain scenery as we head towards our hotel in Lake Garda. Although both Rob and I have been to Italy before – visiting Milan and Lake Como on the last day of a three-week European trek – we have never been to Lake Garda before. It is beautiful, especially the fishing town where we are staying, called Riva, situated at the northernmost tip of the Lakes.

For the next seven days we enjoy idyllic boat trips to the numerous towns dotted around the Lake – Malcesine, Limone and Garda itself. One day we decide to venture further to Venice.

It is such a stunning city and looks even more magical when the sun is shining, illuminating the green-grey canals. We imagine bringing our child here in the future – navigating our way through the maze of pigeons in St. Marks Square and travelling by gondola, as it glides effortlessly past the Bridge of Sighs.

We are both so excited by the next stage of the adoption process that often we find ourselves gazing at families in cafés and restaurants, imagining the day when we will be a family too. But it is hard to picture something that still seems an eternity away. So, until that moment arrives, we decide to make the very most of our time as a couple in one of the most romantic countries in the world. We take the chance to relax – knowing that the next few months will inevitably be challenging. It is a good job we do – for when we return to England to embark on the home study, there is a major problem waiting in the wings.

My medical does not go according to plan.

In fact, it takes almost four weeks for Rob and me to be told whether we can continue with the adoption or not. It turns out to be one of the hardest things we have had to endure so far.

4

The past catches up

JULY–AUGUST 2002

Our home study is to begin just before we have our medicals. Rob and I are allocated to the only male social worker among ten or so women at our adoption agency. He was one of the social workers leading the last workshop and is called Tim. I had predicted as much, though I'm not sure why. A gut feeling, I suppose – as well as the fact that he'd been really friendly and approachable and was of a similar age to us. One or two of the other social workers had seemed more intimidating but we are now tentatively looking forward to starting our home study with Tim as soon as possible.

Tim contacts us to arrange a time to come to our house and run through how the home assessment will work, and how long the whole process will now take. By the time the day arrives for his first home visit, we are both a bundle of nerves again.

Tuesday 2 July 2002
Waking early, we attempt to have breakfast and then head off for an enthusiastic walk with our dogs. We have notified family and friends of the impending meeting, so that they won't ring mid-conversation or leave messages on the

answerphone. We have mugs of tea prepared and biscuits ceremoniously piled high. Now all we have to do is calm ourselves down.

At 11 o'clock, Tim calls to say that he is lost. Somehow we manage to navigate him to our house, and finally our meeting can begin.

First we have to provide passports, utility bills, bank statements, and our marriage certificate for the mandatory police check. Tim tells us that the process, from now until the final adoption panel, will take approximately six months. Today is 2 July, 2002. Tim reckons we will be able to go to panel just before Christmas. What a Christmas present that would turn out to be!

Next we talk in general about what has brought us to the point of adoption and how long we have been thinking about it. We talk a bit about ourselves and we show Tim around our house, telling him about the neighbourhood.

We have not lived here long but Rob and I are already very familiar with the area – both of us having family and friends within walking distance. Nearby there are good local schools, as well as numerous parks and children's play areas. We certainly do not intend to move for many years to come. Having spent a great deal of time decorating the house, particularly our child's-to-be bedroom, we are only too happy to show Tim the finished result. He seems impressed and says that both the house and garden are perfect for any child.

At this point, Tim decides to bring out the Questionnaire for Prospective Adopters, which will provide the basic information for our "Form F".

Nothing can prepare you for this quite mind-boggling set of questions!

Part one deals with individual profiles of each applicant: our education, health, finances and employment histories, our parents, siblings, present relationships and parenting experiences, and our attitudes to ethnicity, religion, disability, abuse, contact with birth families, and behavioural problems! Part two covers more wide-ranging topics to do with our own life stories in relation to the backgrounds of children who need to be adopted, and our capacity to become adoptive parents. I have to say, it seems rather daunting and too much to take in. Tim is aware of our reaction and says that most people feel overwhelmed at first. He talks us through the form and then sets us the first of numerous pieces of homework.

Basically we are asked to answer questions (about fifty of them), on our upbringing, childhood, school life, our talents and emotions, how we cope with stress, loss and change, any significant previous relationships – our last argument and how we resolved it! It leaves us reeling, and we are taken aback at how extremely personal some of the questions appear to be.

Nonetheless, we remain undeterred, as this is what we need to go through for the sake of our adoptive child. We try our best to appear unfazed when we bid Tim goodbye; our next meeting is in two-and-a-half weeks' time.

My medical, meanwhile, is due to take place the very next day. With hindsight, this should undoubtedly have come first.

Wednesday 3 July 2002

I am unprepared for the dredging through of my medical records. No page is left unturned; all thirty-seven years of my life are displayed before me; many ailments or conditions that have completely slipped my mind.

The doctor is supportive of the adoption but says that events from years gone by might prove something of a stumbling block.

The big problem turns out to be that I had psychiatric treatment in my late teens. I had suffered a traumatic event, and my subsequent erratic and abnormal behaviour is seen to be a major setback. It is debatable whether the adoption process can actually proceed any further.

To my mind – and for everyone else who knows me –

this is an extreme reaction. Seventeen years have passed and the issues that haunted me in my late teens are no longer able to affect or blight my life in any way. I would be a perfectly capable mother – and do not feel that I should be judged on a single adolescent episode.

Whilst we wait to hear from the agency's medical advisor, Robbie and I have the second of our home visits from our social worker.

Thursday 18 July 2002

Tim has already warned me that he will have to ask a lot of questions about the troubling episode in my past, and he will then have to add a report to my medical. The next part of our conversation is to be about my infertility and how it affected our relationship – and at what point we decided to adopt. The final part of our chat today will be about our finances and employment situation; no problems there at least!

I can't pretend that the discussion is easy. At times I really feel as though I am baring my soul to a complete stranger. Tim does not make it hard for me to talk about my psychiatric treatment – but neither does he offer any words of encouragement, sitting very much "on the fence" with regard to how the adoption agency's doctor will view the situation. Indeed, at one point he suggests that perhaps we should think seriously about whether or not we wish to continue with our adoption application as we are having to live with such uncertainty and unrest.

Neither Robbie nor I see this as a particularly helpful way of looking at things, and we find it extremely disheartening.

From the time our medical reports are sent to the agency to the time when we have a decision is almost four weeks. That may not sound much when you see it written down, but it seems like an eternity at the time.

So, when the medical adviser finally gives us the OK to go ahead – seeming less concerned about the psychiatric treatment and far more worried about my smoking – the news is met with undeniable relief from us both.

I don't think our social worker has fully understood what we have been through. To cope with infertility and decide to adopt, only to be turned down for something that happened years previously, would have been an almighty blow. I have always felt that it was God's will for Robbie and me to adopt; it was therefore hard to try and make sense of why things could be going so wrong. Fortunately everybody's prayers are answered, and we can continue with the home study feeling a little more positive about the whole thing.

Tuesday 6 August 2002

At this next meeting Tim acknowledges that we have had a difficult start and says that he hopes things will be easier for us in the next few months. I find myself warming to him and really feel he is beginning to understand us.

The meeting, at our London agency this time, will involve Rob and me having hour-long "interrogations" on our own. Something I have not been looking forward to. But first we go over our homework. Our last task was answering questions on our present relationship. We therefore assume that we will have to enlarge on our answers to questions such as:

Describe the most difficult patches of your relationship. (Probably going through the adoption process!)

What led to them and how did you resolve them?

What was your last argument about? How do each of you deal with disagreements and how quickly are they resolved?

What do each of you do that irritates the other?

How do you deal with differences in your sexual needs? Are these resolved? What adjustments have you had to make in your sexual relationship?

Fairly personal questions – almost bordering on intrusive. Undoubtedly, a lot of them are relevant in some way or another, although they were not always easy to answer. However, the questions regarding sexual needs seem unnecessary. I do think that our sex life should be our own affair and nobody else's. I think Tim agrees – judging by the way he was squirming in his seat whilst talking about our answers!

The second part of our homework relates to our support networks; we were asked to design a map showing how close family and friends live to us, and how much we would be able to turn to them for emotional and practical help. It has been a useful exercise and makes us look at local nurseries and pre-school playgroups in our area too. Rob and I enjoy discussing this map with Tim, who seems pleased with all of our research. He is certainly far more relaxed on his own territory, which makes it a whole lot easier to talk and there aren't nearly so many pregnant pauses.

Next on the agenda are the individual chats. Rob is first, so I have to amuse myself for an hour; the staff at the adoption agency try to make me feel at home.

In general, the private conversations deal with subjects we have looked at before – childhood, teenage years, jobs we have done – that sort of thing. For Robbie it is also the first time he has had to talk about a painful bereavement in his family – the death of his father when he was a child. Although Rob finds the subject difficult, he feels that Tim handles the situation well. They discuss past relationships, and Tim also touches on the age difference between us, something that has not really been mentioned before. Robbie simply reiterates what we have always found as a couple – that the age difference (eight years) has absolutely no bearing on our relationship whatsoever. In fact, most people don't really notice or think it is of any great importance. For Tim, I think, it is more a case of Robbie being quite young to adopt – certainly in comparison with the other couples in the workshop. This is true, but twenty-nine is hardly too young to become a father when life's

37

experiences have made you mature beyond your years. Rob would be a fantastic dad and he is as enthusiastic to adopt as I am.

Soon it is my turn for the individual chat and it proves to be nowhere near as daunting as I'd imagined.

We start by covering fairly old ground – my childhood and my teenage years and how I view them now. In the main my childhood was a happy one, my mother and father working hard to give us the best in life. My older brother, Mark, and I were quite spoilt but firmly disciplined too. Mark and I were no angels and had the normal petty quarrels that any siblings have. My teenage years were more problematic and, without immense patience from my family, especially my mother, I would probably have gone far more astray than I did. Having strived to be the perfect student, I suddenly rebelled against "the system". Desperate to shed the image of an "academic", I became quite self-destructive, directing feelings of anger at myself in an attempt to be accepted and fit in with "the crowd". With the help of anti-depressants and therapy I worked through my problems. I hope that at least my difficult adolescence will give me an inkling of how an adopted child might feel when approaching puberty and adulthood.

Tim and I also discuss my religious beliefs and my hobbies, including writing; no comment is made when I tell him about keeping this diary! All in all it is a relaxed, informal chat, and when Rob joins us at the end of the session, Tim seems entirely satisfied with all that we've had to say.

We set about arranging our next meeting – again it will be our turn to come to London. Tim then sets us more homework: we have to examine our lifestyle in relation to becoming a family with children.

Our next appointment is made for 22 August. It will be our fourth so far. Initially Tim said that he expected the home study to take around seven or eight sessions. We will soon be half way through the assessment. We can hardly believe it.

Thursday 22 August 2002

Writing about our family lifestyle has been easy: answering a variety of questions on leisure activities in and out of the home, friends and how much they visit, our attitude to food and nutrition, family celebrations and plans for any religious upbringing of the children. At today's meeting we will be discussing all that we have written, as well as looking at the last piece of homework we submitted: looking at our relationship together.

As we arrive at the agency in an altogether calmer state of mind, Tim greets us warmly and seems keen to do business.

We begin by talking about how we first met (at work, friends for four years, then platonic flat-sharers – then not-so-platonic flat sharers!). It is nice chatting about our first home together, then our wedding day, a gloriously hot May day in 1997 and all the subsequent years since. We discuss difficult patches in our relationship; for us it was having neighbours from hell, and obviously our infertility problems. We also look at the way we deal with arguments and decision-making in our relationship.

We talk about our individual roles within the marriage and the ways in which we let the other one know how much we care; how affection, approval and disapproval are expressed in our home and we look at religion again and my hope to take our child to church. We chat about our personal interests and hobbies and how much television we watch, the sort of food we eat – pasta, chicken, fish, pizza, how we envisage spending the school holidays, and we reiterate how much time we would spend with family and friends.

We talk for almost two hours and the time passes quickly. We do find the question regarding the death of either partner particularly hard to answer. Personally, I would be devastated if anything happened to Rob and I'm sure I would need a lot of support and help with our child in order to pull through. Robbie feels exactly the same way and I think Tim is perfectly aware of it. He simply states that nobody expects us to be superhuman, just to answer the question as honestly as we feel we can.

Tim explains the next piece of homework – probably one of the most important to date. We are about to start looking at part two of the adoption questionnaire, the part that assesses the possible placement and post-placement needs of the child and the adoptive family.

We must start to consider the backgrounds and the events that may have led to children being taken into care in the first place. And we have to look at the particular circumstances we feel we can – and cannot – accept, such as a history of mental ill health or a child who was born through rape or incest. We have to examine the effect that separation from the birth family has on a child (monumental, one would imagine) and also the effect that a complete lack of attachment to adults will have on an eventual placement (difficulties in bonding, naturally). We have to discuss our hopes for our child in the future and our greatest fears about adopting (our child never growing to love us, being my biggest fear). We must also explore our attitude to routine in a child's life, as well as discipline and family rules. We should draw upon our own childhood experiences and discuss the things we would hope to repeat with our child – and those things we would wish to change.

The homework sounds both interesting and challenging and we cannot wait to get started. We spend a long time thinking about our answers; we know that whatever we write down will have a huge impact on the kind of child that may be placed with us in the future. When Tim comes to visit us again in two weeks' time, we must feel clear in our minds about the sort of issues we can deal with.

It is a stressful but exciting stage in the process. Both Rob and I really begin to feel as though we are taking mighty big strides towards our ultimate goal. With every meeting that passes, we are one step closer to becoming approved adopters and fulfilling our dream of becoming parents. We are one step closer to meeting our child: the as yet unknown "you" to whom this diary is dedicated, as a loving gift.

5

Our home study goes on

SEPTEMBER–NOVEMBER 2002

Friends and family keep asking whether it gets easier as the process goes on – whether it becomes more natural opening up to a virtual stranger, sitting opposite you, frantically scribbling notes while remaining non-committal about what you say. The answer is 'yes' and 'no'.

Yes, because we are getting used to this situation and feel that we are getting to know our social worker better and better. No, because the nerves always kick in pre-visit and we are always scared that we are going to say something inappropriate, and completely upset the applecart! We do feel, however, that Tim is working on our side now, and that counts for a lot. We like him and trust his opinions, which is crucial in being able to feel comfortable discussing such personal information. Now that Rob and I have reached this stage in our home study, the focus has switched from us to the child, "our child", and that is an infinitely better place to be.

Friday 6 September 2002

This is session five. When Tim arrives at our house we begin by looking at the issues surrounding a child coming into care – and exactly why he or she is being placed for adoption. Rob and I have done our homework and we have a very clear idea of the sort of backgrounds we can accept and those we cannot. We feel we cannot deal with a history of mental illness in the family, mainly due to the hereditary factors of illnesses like schizophrenia. We also feel that we cannot take a child where little or nothing is known about the birth parents. In the first place, we would find telling that to our child extremely hard – imagine never knowing anything about your start in life and never having any roots to speak of. Personally, I think such lack of information would affect me badly. As much as our heart might be telling us to take the baby left on the doorstep, our head would be telling us to beware. Secondly, without information about the birth parents, it would be impossible to know whether there was a history of mental illness, or any other illness for that matter.

We do feel, however, that we are well prepared to take on a child who has been neglected or physically abused and, as it often goes hand-in-hand, perhaps also sexually abused.

We think that a child should be aware that they are adopted from a young age, so that the subject is never made into a secret suddenly sprung on them at a later stage. But we think that discussing the finer points of why they came into care should be left until they are old enough to comprehend such matters, when professional help might also be needed. Having met a girl who was told at sixteen that she was the product of a father–daughter relationship, I know only too well how such news can send someone crashing off the rails. Information like that must be handled skilfully and sensitively, or the consequences can be dire.

Tim accepts our views without question and leads us into talking about children of mixed heritage.

As Robbie and I are both white Caucasian, it would normally be expected that we would adopt a child of white ethnicity. We state clearly that we would welcome a child of dual heritage – say half-Mediterranean or Irish and half-British. This, we gather, is acceptable if we can "promote an awareness" of the child's culture through visits and books and general knowledge. However, we will not be able to adopt a child with dual heritage if we cannot "actively reflect" the child's ethnicity and culture in our everyday lives. So partly African-Caribbean or Asian children will not be placed with us, seeing as our family and friends are nearly all white.

At first I have a problem accepting this fact, as do so many other prospective adopters. When I was growing up, I knew black children who had been adopted into white households, with little or no difficulties at all. Nowadays this is generally discouraged, as research has revealed that black or mixed-race children may lose some of their sense of identity and roots if brought up in a mainly white environment. Understandably, I suppose, this could lead to resentment as the child grows older and to a feeling of not really belonging. Studies have shown that placing "mixed-race" children with "mixed-race" parents has a more beneficial effect than placing them with white carers. I just question the number of older "mixed-race" and black children who have been left in care for many years because there have not been enough suitable adopters coming forward.

At least, based on our experiences at the workshop in May, it seems that more families of mixed ethnicity now want to adopt children who would otherwise remain in foster homes or children's homes for a very long time indeed.

Physical disability is next, and both Rob and I feel we could help a child with a hearing loss or visual impairment (having done a substantial amount of work with the blind myself). We are open to discussing a range of other minor disabilities, but would have to draw the line, from a practical point of view, on any mobility restrictions, as I do not drive. This would apply to any conditions that required a great deal of medical support at the hospital. Rob works full-time, and it would not always be possible for me to provide the necessary transport if, say, our child was in a wheelchair. Tim seems happy with all that we have said and writes copious notes.

Children's behavioural problems and learning disabilities present a much greyer area. I find myself feeling a touch guilty and quite embarrassed at admitting that there are certain things I cannot cope with. Tim keeps reminding me that it is perfectly OK to say 'no', as it is far better to be honest from the start than try to pretend that we can deal with anything at all.

Severe autism or Attention Deficit Hyperactivity Disorder (ADHD) are two problems we feel could be too much of a challenge for us. We understand that not every child will have been diagnosed with these conditions before being placed for adoption, and therefore, like for any birth parent, there will have to be an element of the unknown, and we are ready to accept that. What we are saying, however, is that if the diagnosis has already been made, then we would not wish to adopt those children. Sounds harsh, I know, but it is necessary for us to accept our limitations.

Tim is in full agreement. The last thing he wants is for us to say that we can cope with something if we clearly cannot. The discussion is frank and sometimes difficult, but it is one of the main parts of the assessment to date.

Having spent the best part of two hours on heavy issues, all of us are in need of a break. Robbie and I feel that we have made real headway with the whole adoption process.

Apparently, we are not wrong either. Robbie asks how many meetings are left before we complete our home study. By our calculations we reckon we have two or three, as Tim originally told us that the assessment would take between seven or eight sessions – and so far we have completed five. We are therefore amazed (and delighted!), when Tim informs us that we should be able to wrap the whole thing up in one more session – making our home assessment a grand total of six meetings in all!

I have to admit that at first I am so taken aback that I actually start to wonder whether we have covered all the necessary subjects in enough detail. It seems to me that we have spent an inordinate amount of time discussing us as a couple and as individuals, but the most important part, that of discussing the adopted child, has been dealt with rather hastily. Rob and I consider this at length and realise that, in fact, most aspects have been studied and talked through, apart from contact with the birth family, which is to be covered next time. We are almost incredulous that it is now happening so quickly. When we share the news with our family and friends, everyone is as exited as we are. It is one of the more exhilarating times in the adoption process – and one that I allow myself to savour.

Not for long, however. The much anticipated last session is not quite the final crescendo we have been hoping for, as we are soon given some rather new and depressing facts.

Wednesday 25 September 2002
The session starts rather well. We have travelled to London again for this all-important last interview, and Tim is in good form, asking us if there is anything from the last meeting that we feel we need to pursue. We say we are happy to go on and begin by looking at how much contact with the child's birth family we are prepared to accept and facilitate.

Although we still feel reluctant to have face-to-face contact with the birth parents, Rob and I have agreed that we would encourage contact with siblings if our child has any brothers or sisters. It would be dependent on geographical factors – if a brother had been adopted in Scotland for instance, then this would determine how often we could arrange a meeting. Generally, contact seems to take place annually, or twice yearly, which would be fine with us. We are also open to letterbox contact with birth parents once a year, and with any grandparents or perhaps a favourite aunt who may wish to send a message every so often. Both of us think that letterbox contact is a good idea, because it would enable our child to ask questions to which we might not have all the answers. But we feel that when a child is old enough to make up their own mind, then it should be up to them whether they wish to continue with letterbox or with direct contact.

Now we learn about the complexity of actually being matched with a child in the first place. Tim shows us the "profiles" of three or four children who need to be adopted. All of them are gorgeous and all the details are quite glowing – a little too much so, in fact, as Tim is quick to point out. What shocks us, however, is that beside each child's details is a list of prospective adopters already interested in that particular child and the "books" aren't even closed yet! In effect, what this means for us is that when our social worker gives us a ring to say that he thinks he may have found a child for us we will not be the only family given details of that child. We may, in fact, be one of five, ten or even twenty families all vying for the same child. Nobody told us that at the workshops back in May!

It makes sense, of course, if you look at it from the child's point of view. The child's social worker distributes the details to many different social services departments, adoption agencies and publications such as *Be My Parent* and *Adoption Today*. That way the social worker has the best possible likelihood of finding a suitable family for the child – and that must be everybody's main concern.

What is quite tough is the knowledge that we may get down to the last ten couples, then five; we may see a video of the child and meet the child's social workers and we may even make the shortlist of the last two couples; only then will our linking report go to panel to see who is regarded as the most suitable match. At this late stage we could be told that the panel has chosen the other couple. How devastating would that be? Absolutely heartbreaking – and these situations can and do happen regularly.

We are told, quite calmly, not to build our hopes up at any stage; to remain emotionally detached from the children whose "profiles" we will be seeing.

This is asking the impossible when you have already endured years of infertility. It is a very tough call indeed.

The next slightly depressing bit of news we hear is that when a child is eventually placed with a family, it can take up to a year before the court makes an Adoption Order. During that time the child will not be able to take our name legally, though at nursery or school, for example, it would be perfectly OK for them to answer to our surname. We will not be able to apply for a passport or give consent if our child needs an operation or other medical treatment, without getting agreement from social services first.

Also, as Tim says, it means that for up to a year we will be having social workers visit our house to see how we are doing. Once a month, if everything is going well; once a fortnight, if there are any problems.

We can hardly wait.

So it seems that as much as we want to look forward, there is always something around the corner that comes along to dampen the spirits.

Tim does try to keep our enthusiasm from waning. He points out that as Rob and I are hoping to adopt a two-to five-year-old rather than an infant, we will probably have less of a wait for our child, and more children to choose from. We are also happy to have either a boy or a girl, another advantage, as more people want a girl. Tim tells us that, although one of his couples has been waiting over a year for a child, not all matches take so long, some only a matter of months.

From personal experience, Robbie and I know a couple who took a mere four months to be linked with the right child. On the other hand, we also know of a couple who went through eighteen months of hell before finally having their little girl – so we really cannot know what will happen. What I do know is that, no matter how long it takes, it will be so very worthwhile in the end. Our son or daughter is out there somewhere – not yet knowing that soon they will become part of our family, their "forever family" – and we will wait until they come to us.

As this last session draws to a close, we are thankful that we have finished our part of the home study.

Tim explains that the next thing for him to do is visit two of our closest friends to discuss their written references, and have more of a general chat about us as a couple.

Both of our friends are anxious about the forthcoming interviews, and no one can blame them for that! It is a big responsibility for anyone to undertake and we agree that it is a shame that they've had to wait until the end of the home study, as sooner would have been better.

As it turns out, each meeting goes without a hitch. Trevor, a longstanding college friend of Rob's, gives a wonderful reference, having worked with us both for many years and knowing our personalities well. One of my best friends, Liz, gets on so well with our social worker that Tim says he feels he has known her for years! She talks at length about our years of infertility and how we have come to accept that we will never have our own birth child. She repeats how much she supports the adoption and knows it is what we both want. Having known us both for over a decade (we were neighbours first, then friends), Liz says she is sure we will be conscientious and caring parents. Both of our friends will see a lot of our child when he or she is placed with us and they can feel justifiably proud that they have played an important part in the whole adoption process.

The third reference lies in the capable hands of my mother. Tim does not have to visit her (surprising, I thought), he just needs a letter. As ever, my mum delivers a beautiful and heartfelt response – she is overjoyed at the prospect of another grandchild in the family.

Now the only thing left to do is wait. We imagine that there will be an awful lot of this to do, so we try to function as normally as possible, while all the time knowing that a panel date to hear our application could soon be arranged.

Tim now has to write up our full F1 form, which will be sent to us at home to read and sign and return to the head of the agency. Then he will apply for a slot at the next available adoption panel meeting, which he is very much hoping will be before Christmas. We have our final two-day workshop coming up in London on 22 and 23 November. It would be great to have the panel date soon after that – although we are definitely not building up our hopes.

Saturday 16 November 2002

It turns out that we did not make the November panel date, as there were so many people waiting already. Tim informs us that we have been pencilled in for the December panel, but warns us that date could be postponed until the New Year. We really hope not – though in our heart of hearts that is exactly what we are expecting to happen. Although we feel a little frustrated, the delay is entirely understandable and nobody's fault. It would be so nice though, to be finally approved.

In the meantime, we simply wait some more. We fill in questionnaires on our dogs: one form per dog, each containing some rather ridiculous questions, twenty-eight in all, to be precise. We also ring to enquire after some children featured in the *Be My Parent* magazine – nothing comes of it, but sometimes even getting to talk to a social worker about a child seems an achievement in itself!

We decide to focus all our attentions on the two more forthcoming workshops, which are less than a week away now. We read through the proposed itinerary and two anonymised "Form Es" (soon to change to "Form CPR (Child Permanence Report)" under new legislation) which are sent to us, containing information on two children who need adoption. It all sounds very interesting. We are hoping to learn a lot more about the actual placement of a child, the legal proceedings, and what happens in court. We are also very much wanting to hear more adoptive parents' stories. Everything seems so much more real and personal at first hand.

Will these workshops really be the last piece of the jigsaw before we are finally approved as adopters? It is an exciting time for us both and we aim to enjoy it.

6

The final workshops

NOVEMBER–DECEMBER 2002

It hardly seems possible that our home assessment has finished and here we are, about to embark on our final adoption workshops.

Feeling far less nervous than in May, we are hoping to catch up with the other adopters and to compare our different experiences so far. It will be interesting to see how people have fared over the past six months.

Friday 22 November 2002
Day 1 of the workshops: the first thing that strikes us as we enter the room is that there are fewer familiar faces than we have been anticipating. Five couples are missing. We hear that one couple has seen their application turned down, and the others have either given up, been discouraged or are at a different stage in the process to us.

There are some faces we do know, and it is great to see people again and find out what they have thought of the assessment so far.

One "mixed-race" couple has already been to panel and they are now approved adopters – which makes them feel very positive. Another older couple, both in their early fifties, are waiting to adopt an eight-to ten-year-old – so it is interesting to talk to them, as many adopters will only consider very young children. One couple seem notably disillusioned and depressed by the whole thing. Being fed negative stories and hearing of the very worst-case scenarios has taken its toll, and they tell us they feel despondent and disheartened. They have gone to the trouble of seeking out an Adoption Support Group to try and talk through their difficulties. But instead of reassuring them, the group has filled them with even more doom and gloom, with extremely negative stories. As our social worker points out, although it can prove helpful to join a support group, it is not much use if you only hear about the problems, which may, in some instances, be grossly exaggerated. I'm sure that for many adopters these groups are invaluable. My main worry is that in a lot of cases the people most likely to attend will be those experiencing the greatest difficulties. For someone about to go to panel for approval, it doesn't always seem the best thing to do, especially if you're hoping to keep some enthusiasm alive! Maybe adopters with happy stories simply do not make the time to go to these meetings. It's something to be aware of if you are hoping to hear tales of joy.

It is a pleasant surprise to see Tim, our social worker, taking Friday's course. We begin by looking at linking children with families and the sorts of questions the child's social worker may ask. They are daunting to say the least.

How would you cope with adolescent problems?

How would you cope with stealing and lying?

How do you feel about tantrums in public?

How would you feel if your son started masturbating in Woolworths? (Apart from pretend he isn't mine, you mean.)

Everyone shuffles in their seats uncomfortably. I cannot help but think that many of these things would worry you about a birth child, as well as an adopted child. And again, I am slightly concerned that we only seem to be looking at the negatives of parenthood.

We now look together at the two Form Es, sent to us before the course, which give details about children needing family placement, such as medical conditions, family, social and educational histories, matching criteria, contact needs and the legal situation. They also have a list of the child's placements since birth, a profile of the child and information on the birth parents and siblings, if known.

These are the types of forms we will see when a real child is finally discussed with us. But they could, quite easily, be almost a year out of date by the time we read them. For a three-year-old, that is a large proportion of his or her life; a large proportion which has not been fully documented (though medical reports, at least, should not be more than six months out of date).

Another important point, illustrated by a role-playing exercise in groups, is that social workers may not necessarily have all of the answers to all of our questions. The child's worker may have changed more than once and there may have been a general lack of continuity, so that an amount of uncertainty has to be considered normal.

The role-playing exercise shows us that not all the information about a child may be available before placement and that some of the relevant facts may be misunderstood. Robbie and I know of two adoptive families where important information only came to light either just before the match was approved or, in one case, only after the child was already living with the adopters. Both families worked through their problems, but would have appreciated more information much earlier on in the process. It is worth noting that a couple has won a partial victory against Essex county council for non-disclosure of facts regarding their adopted son. They have been awarded damages in court, thereby setting a precedent for the future and hopefully ensuring that social workers are as open and honest as possible when sharing information about children placed for adoption.

The afternoon session is fascinating and an informative couple of hours, although it is also rather negative. A play therapist speaks to us about her work and shows us various games that we can play to encourage a traumatised child to talk about feelings. Puppets are a big hit with children of most ages; young children especially find talking to "teddy" easier than talking to the new adults in their life.

The play therapist spends much of her time dealing specifically with traumatised children who have come from difficult backgrounds and have been abused. She uses a chart to depict the first six months of a placement. We are told how the child will go through a honeymoon period followed by anger, mistrust and, possibly, depression. By the time the child has hit the depressive stage – the "pits" of depression is the phrase actually used – we, as parents, could have sunk into an even deeper depression just as we are called upon to be strong.

Now I realise that the therapist is reporting from her practice, but neither Rob nor I find these messages particularly encouraging, although I understand that we must be prepared for worst-case scenarios.

Feeling pretty flat by now, I am fortunate because I have been able to talk to a woman who has adopted four children and felt exactly the same as us about never hearing positive accounts of adoption, nearly always having to look at the negative aspects. There have been problems with each of her placements but none were quite as horrific as they'd been led to expect. She emphasised that the sheer joys they have experienced so far more than outweigh the difficulties.

We hope the next day will be less intense and help us to end on a positive note.

Saturday 23 November 2002
One of the high points of the day is an adoptive couple coming in to talk about their experience – and their story could so easily have had a disastrous outcome. Their two

adopted children witnessed an appalling crime when they were very young. The result of this crime was that they were left without both a mother and a father. With the help of therapists and support from our adoption agency and their own network of family and friends, the adoptive parents have completely transformed the lives of these two troubled children. As Tim himself puts it, they have worked miracles.

One of the other main issues covered on Day 2 (and something that Tim subsequently talks through with us at length) is managing introductions. This is the intensive two to three week "handover" period before a child eventually comes to live in your home.

Having spoken to adopters who have "been there and done it", this does sound an exhausting time – both emotionally and physically. A major factor is the distance between where the prospective adopters and the child and foster family live. If you live in Birmingham and are being linked with a child in Dorset, then you are going to need to stay over at a guesthouse and make suitable arrangements for any birth children who may be at home and not travelling with you. For us, it would mean sorting out something for our dogs.

Apparently the first day we go to meet our child-to-be, the visit normally lasts an hour or so. This will build up over the weeks until eventually we will be arriving in the morning to wake, dress and have breakfast with the child – and spend the day together and put them to bed. We might even have them to sleep over at our house for a night or two. All this very much depends on the age of the child. For example, the introduction period for a baby is usually shorter than for a three-to four-year-old – for very obvious reasons. Imagine how excruciatingly hard it must be for a child to say goodbye to foster carers or friends, home, pets or anyone or anything they may have become comfortable with, and now have to leave behind. Imagine being told that you are moving to the other end of the country, to a new house, a new family, a new school. It's no wonder introductions have to be handled with extreme sensitivity and understanding on all sides. And how hard it must be for the foster carers.

All together it will prove to be a very testing time for everyone involved. We listen to Tim intently as he tries to indicate how emotional and stressed we might feel at the "introductory" stage. It sounds challenging but is something we both feel prepared for.

So, after much soul-searching and deliberation we are finally at the end of our very last workshop and at the end of our assessment. Rob and I have somehow managed to come through it all and the next, rather interesting stage is for us to be given our completed Form F. We will have to carefully read through it, sign it, and return it to our agency in preparation for going to panel.

So far, so good.

Thursday 28 November 2002

When the completed Form F falls through our letterbox in the morning, I literally rip open the envelope.

It is some seventeen pages long in all and it is both thorough and complimentary. Tim has done an exemplary job and assessed us accurately and warmly, wholeheartedly recommending us for approval at panel. From a social worker who has to remain detached at all times, this is wonderful stuff. Even better is the news that we have been pencilled in for the very last adoption panel of the year – 11 December, 2002!

We are over the moon!

The next two-and-a-half weeks seem the longest in history – the time drags on unbearably. Even though we keep telling ourselves that the actual panel hearing is more of a formality, we cannot help but conjure up all manner of things that could go wrong.

We are thrilled too, don't get me wrong! This, after all, is the moment we have been waiting for. Finally, after a deluge of self-doubt and worry, the day is upon us. The day when we will finally be told whether we are going to be parents after all.

Wednesday 11 December 2002

Different people have very different views as to whether they would like the opportunity to attend their panel meeting or not. I have spoken to adoptive parents who have, and found the experience both fraught and nerve-wracking.

Then again, some people on our course very much wanted the chance to answer any questions that might arise and to feel part of the process. I have to admit that I am rather relieved to be spared the experience because we are not invited. I believe, however, that in due course it is to be made mandatory for adopters to attend when their application is heard. So by the time you read this, it has probably become general practice.

Tim informs us that the panel will consider our application at 9.45am. Each case usually takes anywhere from between thirty to forty-five minutes. He makes it clear that he will not be able to ring us until lunchtime as he is one of the senior social workers who have to sit through the whole meeting.

Knowing that Tim is going to ring us between 12.30 and 1 o' clock is fine.

Actually ringing us some twenty-five minutes late is not!

By then my stomach is in knots and Rob and I are way beyond conversation.

When the phone eventually rings, we both leap up from our seats and I ask Robbie to pick up the receiver, knowing only too well that my voice will break if I answer it.

When Robbie smiles and says, 'That's fantastic news,' I'm not ashamed to say that I cry. Many years of pent-up emotion come flooding over me and the tears do not stop for quite some time.

Tim, our social worker, is genuinely happy for us both

and tells us we deserve to go out and celebrate. It is a truly wonderful moment, and Tim is pleased to tell us that the decision has been unanimous.

The next two hours are spent ringing round family and friends "in waiting" – all hovering by their phones! My parents are both relieved and delighted when I tell them our news. My nephew and niece, Luke and Bethany, run screaming from the phone to tell my brother that they are going to have a new cousin. Rob's mum and sister are absolutely thrilled, as is Rob's eight-year-old niece, Kirsty. Our friends – most of them having supported us for the last ten years – send us congratulatory messages and bottles of champagne.

Days of celebration follow. In fact, it takes almost a week for the news to really sink in: the knowledge that now, almost certainly, we can look forward to the day when we become proud parents of a son or daughter – after almost nine years of waiting. It is a magical time.

All the hard work over the past nine months has finally come to fruition, like a pregnancy. The joy and happiness that we feel is indescribable.

Somewhere out there a child is waiting for us. We are counting the days until we meet "you", for then, at last, we will become your "forever family".

7

A child is waiting

JANUARY–JULY 2003

Remember our sheer delight at being approved at panel in December? Our joy at the thought of becoming parents?

Well, hold on to that feeling – because things change fast.

Nothing, I repeat, nothing is like the fall after panel. The anti-climax of no activity, no structure to work to, no way of telling how long the wait for a child is going to be…The frustration is immense and no amount of preparation is ever going to convey how flat it feels when the excitement of panel day has waned.

Certainly Rob and I felt that there was a general lack of support "post-approval". It did not help that we were assigned a trainee social worker for the first three months after panel. Although a pleasant young woman, we only met her once, and spent the entire time going over old ground. It was clear that she had not read our Form F, our seventeen-page CV; in fact, she actually said as much, which didn't exactly fill us with confidence. We felt as though we were being assessed all over again and we certainly wished that we could be back with Tim, whom we had learned to trust.

Four months passed and absolutely nothing happened.

In that time we shared in a wonderful family Christmas and saw in the New Year full of optimism and anticipation – 2003 was going to be our "special year". So when nothing happened for months on end, neither Rob nor I could quite maintain our initial enthusiasm.

We had been warned that a wait at this stage was likely, but what was a little surprising in our case was the apparent lack of available two-to five-year-olds we could even enquire about.

Our trainee social worker had at first indicated that there would be numerous Form Es (the child's "CV", if you like) for us to think about. She said that the duty officer at our agency often sifted through between four and forty referrals a month.

But there was not one that was considered suitable for Rob and me. Not one in four months, which was disappointing to say the least.

The frustration of waiting became very hard at times and we needed our family and friends to lean on.

I also threw myself into my voluntary work with the blind. I usually visit older people in their homes, helping them to read their post, as well as enjoying a chat and a cup of tea together. One lady, Kath, was a wonderful inspiration for me at this time. She was nearly eighty, blind, immobile and suffering from quite severe dementia. She was also witty, caring, a fabulous story-teller (her tales of the second world war were breathtaking) and she still loved a daily tipple of sherry and a really good gossip! She put everything into perspective for me when the waiting became tough. She, and my husband too, remained towers of strength throughout.

Talking to friends we'd made in the workshops also helped immensely. The "mixed-race" couple, who had already been matched with a little girl, were wonderfully encouraging, lifting our spirits when we needed it most.

Unfortunately the other, older couple we talked to regularly on the phone were having a terrible time of it.

Due to their social worker being somewhat slow, it was taking many months to get through to panel. This seemed an awful waste of time, especially as they were eventually approved to adopt a much older child, and the boy they were "matched" with needed to be placed in a permanent home as soon as possible. As there are far too few people coming forward to adopt older children, aged seven or over, I was amazed that priority was not given to this particular placement.

When Robbie and I travelled to London for our first review meeting in mid-April, we were not expecting the best of news.

Thursday 10 April 2003

Rob and I are glad that our trainee social worker has now served her time working with us. In the few months we have been with her, we feel that time has stood still, though this is not entirely her fault. Nevertheless, it is reassuring to be back with Tim, even if the immediate future is looking a little bleak. When we arrive at our agency it is clear that Tim is as frustrated with the situation as we are.

He explains that local authorities are now managing to place a lot of their children within their own boroughs as many more people are apparently coming forward to adopt. In effect, this means that voluntary agencies, like ours, are not having as many children referred to them, at least not young white children without significant special needs.

Tim warns us that we could be in for quite a wait yet, and both Rob and I go away from the meeting feeling desperately low.

We talk and talk and then I ring round masses of social services departments throughout the country to try and get a feel of the climate. By and by Rob and I come to a decision. We decide that as we have always intended to adopt another child in two or three years, we will widen our search to include siblings, that is, we will ask to go back to panel to be approved to take either one or two children.

Thursday 24 April 2003

We ring Tim. He agrees that in the present circumstances this might be a good move. It seems a sensible decision as we have always imagined having two children one day, and frankly, neither of us knows whether we would really want to go through the whole adoption process a second time.

Tim explains that he will not be able to meet up with us and re-write the final part of the Form F until June (we are now in the last week of April). He says that, hopefully, he will be able to get us back to panel by July, and this time both Rob and I will be required to attend. We have no choice but to accept the situation and try and carry on with our lives as normally as possible.

Friday 2 May 2003

One week later, Tim rings to say that he has the Form E for a little girl whom he thinks we might be interested in. She is two-and-a-half years old, comes from a large group of siblings, and has "issues". We say that we would like to see the Form E regardless, and it turns out to be a fascinating and detailed read of almost twenty pages.

From the outset I think we both know that something does not feel right about this little girl, even though her photograph is quite adorable. She has disturbing behaviour problems and there are complicated contact issues with her birth family. So in our heart of hearts we know that we are not the right family for her.

What has made us sit up and think is the fact that this little girl is of mixed ethnicity – black and white – and we have previously been told, repeatedly, that we cannot be considered for such children.

It appears that in some cases there might be some flexibility after all.

I ring a couple of social services departments to find out

more. One senior social worker informs me that they no longer discriminate against people of a different skin colour. Some local authorities now agree that if a "mixed-race" child could end up staying in care for a long time, then it is better for a white family to be considered as adopters than no families at all.

This seems a far better way of looking after a child's best interests than before. If a white couple or single carer can demonstrate that a child will grow up being enabled to embrace their culture, and mix with children of all ethnic backgrounds, then surely that is an infinitely better proposition for a child than staying in care indefinitely.

But this is when the process of adoption really shows itself to be both unbelievably disheartening and a touch cruel.

Mid-May 2003

Rob and I begin to make tentative enquiries about various children of mixed ethnicity in *Be My Parent* and *Children Who Wait*. It takes seven calls over five days to get to speak to one agency social worker about a particular child.

Then, at last, we think our luck might be changing.

There is a little boy who sounds fabulous. He has been featured several times in one of the magazines, and Rob and I really feel we would like to hear more about him.

I ring and ring and then I email the social worker concerned. Finally we get to speak. I present our case, saying that we have "mixed-race" friends, including the couple from the workshops who have already adopted their little girl.

The social worker is interested enough to ask for our Form F and tells us that she thinks our agency may already have the little boy's Form E.

Well, they did, until Tim decided to shred it two days before we ring him because he didn't consider us for this child! An agonising two weeks then pass before we eventually have the Form E in our hands.

It is very encouraging.

Tim supports us in trying for this little boy and indicates that things look quite promising, as the local authority has been unable to place this child over many months. He explains why he has not sent us the Form E before: initially the child's social worker was adamant that they did not want a white couple. She has been swayed by my persuasive argument over the phone. Friends and family are as hopeful as we are.

When you first embark on the adoption path, you are advised not to get too "drawn in" by a child's photograph. You are advised to remain emotionally detached.

Well, all I can say is that in reality it turns out somewhat different.

When you get that phone call telling you that they have placed "your" child with other adopters (or a single black carer in our case), your heart plummets right through the floor. You just cannot believe it. You are angry that you haven't been warned that you are up against other adopters. You are angry, because the child in this particular case has a white mother, a white foster carer and is described in their Form E as having "fair skin".

It is a huge disappointment. Robbie and I agree that we will have to think very carefully before applying for a "mixed-race" child again. For, as one social worker said to us the day after losing this child, 'You can apply for a mixed-race child, but if mixed-race or black adopters come along, they will nearly always take precedence over a white couple'.

Which only leaves you open to more hurt in the long run.

Although despondent, we eventually pick ourselves up and carry on. We decide to go on holiday to Iceland, which is somewhere we have always wanted to explore.

Saturday 24 May – 31 May 2003

Flying into Iceland is an experience in itself. The landscape can only be described as "lunar" – so desolate and barren that you almost begin to wonder whether anyone lives there at all.

Then, when you journey to Reykjavik and are greeted by a brightly coloured and lively young city (complete with imported trees), you realise that the country is one of stark contrasts.

The scenery is nothing short of spectacular. Massive glaciers combine with amazing waterfalls, cavernous craters, bubbling mud pools and explosive geysers – which shoot high above your head. The thermally heated Blue Lagoon is set slap-bang in the middle of nowhere – and is the most relaxing "bath" that Robbie and I have ever had the pleasure to experience.

The holiday is a much-needed boost to the system and when we return home (considerably poorer – Reykjavik is not cheap!), we feel ready to start over again.

The annoying thing about having such a great holiday is having to return to the reality of the "waiting game". We had, in fact, been given information on a little girl a couple of days before we went to Iceland. We study her details more thoroughly on our return.

This child is three-and-a-half years old and from all that Tim has been told, he feels we would be good parents for her. He has already sent our Form F to the local authority in question. Tim says we should soon have a response – though, of course, things never run according to plan.

Tim has warned us that some social workers seem to work to a different timescale. He complains how hard it makes his own job sometimes when no one will return a call or it takes months to arrange a meeting. It makes me feel quite sorry for the position Tim is in. He has approved adopters, like us, repeatedly ringing him, clearly upset at not hearing anything for weeks on end – and all the time he's feeling the same frustration as we are! As he says to us on more than one occasion, nothing would make him happier than being able to place children as quickly as possible, but the "system" simply doesn't work that way.

Early June 2003
After what seems like an eternity of waiting (and numerous more questions from the little girl's social worker), we are told that the child's social services department wishes to proceed with us. We begin to feel elated once again.

We are duly sent the little girl's Form E.

Annie sounds absolutely lovely. And because there isn't a photo attached to her profile, we can make the decision to go on without being swayed by what she looks like. I almost prefer it that way – it helps us to remain just that little bit detached. The really exciting bit comes when Tim lets us know that Annie's family placement worker and Annie's social worker, whom I have spoken to on the phone, want to come and meet us. This meeting is to decide whether Robbie and I will be selected for Annie, or whether the other family being considered (we are the two families on the shortlist) will be the "victors". I deliberately use the word "victors" because the whole set up is so tinged with competitiveness, that we are made to feel it is a duel.

The date for the visit is set for 2 July. Then the local authority contacts Tim to change the date to 10 July. We are assured that the other family will have already been seen by then, thus allowing the final decision to be made quickly, rather than drawing it out over several weeks.

The build up to the meeting is madness. We are a bundle of different emotions, as are all our family and friends. Much as we try and carry on with our everyday life, we cannot help but wonder, most of the time, whether we are one step closer to having our own child. Robbie and I live only twenty miles away from the town where Annie lives with her foster family. It is a place we often visit, and to know that there is a child living there who could one day be our daughter makes it very hard indeed to remain calm.

Thursday 10 July 2003

When the day finally arrives for our meeting, Robbie and I are as prepared as we are ever going to be. We have had so many good luck phone calls that the receiver is red hot. We have also spoken to our friends who adopted their little girl in February, and they have been full of handy hints and reassuring words.

Tim arrives an hour before Annie's social workers. He seems very positive about the whole thing. We run through a lot of the questions he knows we will be asked and we also discuss the sort of questions we are going to be asking – medical questions and points of general interest. Surprisingly, neither Robbie nor I are as tense as we thought we'd be. The house is looking tidy but not too tidy – still "homely" and inviting for a child. We have even started clearing away things that are not particularly child-friendly. All in all it is safe to say that we are feeling quietly confident about the meeting and are extremely keen to hear more about this lovely little girl.

After a late arrival, we can begin. Sarah, the family placement worker, is both pleasant and friendly, although Annie's social worker, Karen, is more restrained and aloof. Both women introduce themselves to Tim, with whom there have been many phone calls over the past few weeks. Then they want to meet our two dogs; they seem impressed with their behaviour.

Next comes the tour of the house, of which Sarah in particular approves. Finally, we all sit ourselves around our large dining table, and I set about preparing drinks and cakes.

The questioning, when it starts, is mainly from us. Too much so, we feel, and although several matters are touched upon, neither of us regard the discussion as "in depth" enough.

One cause of our concern is that the other family being considered already has a child. We have no idea whether this will go in their favour or whether, in fact, it will benefit us; Annie specifically needs one-on-one attention according to her Form E.

Sarah and Karen stay with us for a little under ninety minutes. We have been told that the meeting will probably take two to three hours, so either we have done well in a shorter time, or else they are not really interested.

Sarah does make some very positive comments. She says that we are insightful, caring people who have given Annie's needs and wishes a great deal of thought. Karen adds that we will make wonderful parents to either Annie or any other child, but as she has spent most of the meeting with a look of scarcely concealed boredom, it feels as though she is reading from a script.

At the end of the meeting, Robbie and I make the very hard decision not to look at a photo of Annie, just in case we are not the "chosen" family. We are actually advised not to look at it and we are told that the other family has not seen it either.

I do feel quite let down at this point. I had so wanted to see Annie's face (possibly my daughter's face, to put it in perspective). The fact that we are getting very strong messages that it would not be the right thing to do sends alarm bells ringing.

Before the meeting, we truly thought that we might stand a chance of becoming parents to this little girl.

Now, my gut reaction is, that we do not.

Robbie is not sure and Tim seems more positive than either one of us, but even he is not entirely convinced. He tells us that it could not have gone any better and how pleased he is that we managed to control our nerves and were just "ourselves" – the best bit of advice I could pass on to anyone. We know that we will have an answer from Sarah within seven or eight days at the latest, and that those few days will seem like years and be pure emotional torture.

Thursday 17 July 2003

When we get a phone call saying that we have not been selected, we feel as if our whole world has just caved in around us.

When we find out that the decision has been based largely on budget – not having to pay a voluntary agency to move Annie from her existing borough – we start to feel more than a little angry. Especially when we realise that the child will be remaining in the same town, same area, same nursery school. So if birth mum (presently on walkabout) ever does come back, she will know exactly where to find her daughter.

As Tim makes clear, this is not in the best interests of the child.

We question whether the visit to us was serious in the first place. It rather looks as though the decision had been made even before they came to see us; Rob and I merely making up the numbers, as this particular local authority likes to make the final choice between two families.

We are angry and upset, not only for us, but also for our family and friends, who are equally disappointed. It is almost as heartbreaking for me to hear the pain in my mother's voice, as it is to confront my own anguish.

If we had been told that the other family was selected because they had more childcare experience or because they already had a child, then we would have accepted the decision with some grace and assumed it would be best for Annie.

When money becomes part of the equation, then you have to start asking yourself whether everything is really done for the sake of the child. Especially when Annie's social workers ring Tim a few days later, to ask if they can keep us "on hold" just in case the placement "goes wrong" with the other family.

This doesn't exactly show immense confidence in their choice of family. And it shows an appalling disregard for human emotion – wanting to keep us dangling on a string.

And how much do Annie's feelings count in all of this?

Tim tells them that their "request" is not acceptable. None of us feel that we would want to work with this department again. So it is a case of accepting what has happened and moving on, before bitterness can take hold. Sadly, it is just not meant to be – Annie is not the child for us after all.

However, time does not stand still for long. Prayers do get answered, even when we might begin to doubt.

Within ten days of losing Annie, Tim contacts us with the details of another child. A little boy, not yet turned three, and his name is Peter.

He sounds great, his social workers are keen to get on, and, even better, we are the only couple being considered for him at this time.

Could this little boy really end up being "the one", we ask ourselves over and over again. Might we have a son waiting for us?

We can only dare to hope.

We can only dare to dream.

8

Is Peter our son?

JULY–OCTOBER 2003

The previous six months have proved to be something of an emotional rollercoaster. Rob and I are beginning to wonder how we would cope if we suffer too many more crushing disappointments. We know it will become harder and harder to pick ourselves up and start all over again.

Meanwhile, we both wait impatiently for Peter's Form E to come in the post. We know that his social worker is keen and we pray that we aren't going to be let down again, so soon after losing Annie.

Friday 25 July 2003
Peter's Form E arrives on a gloriously sunny morning – a good omen, we feel. We rush to open it and Robbie takes a quick look before leaving for work. Then I read it thoroughly from start to finish.

Before long I am ringing Rob at work to discuss various points of interest in the form. There is nothing in the detailed report that either of us finds troubling – Peter sounds like a normal, playful, stubborn, mischievous and lovable little boy. He sounds like our son.

We are also thrilled that he is still comparatively young – turning three in a few months, in late autumn. We ring

Tim to confirm that we wish to proceed. Things then move so fast that it all becomes a bit of a blur.

Within hours Tim is ringing us back to tell us that Peter's social worker, Clare, would like to come down to meet us the following Thursday. As this means a three-hour drive, we figure she must really like the sound of us!

We are so excited all over again, as is my mother who has remained quietly optimistic throughout and comforted me whenever I have nearly felt like giving up. Is our son really waiting for us out there? Peter, can you ever begin to realise how much we want you to be part of our family?

We start to believe that our luck is really about to change. Dare we allow ourselves to think so positively while perhaps heading for yet another fall? It is certainly difficult to stay composed at such a time, and we cannot help but build our hopes up once again.

Thursday 31 July 2003
Then, before we know it, the following Thursday is upon us.

We are both stressed – more so than at our ill-fated meeting, some two weeks earlier. That meeting has left a nasty taste in our mouths and we are desperate not to let anything cloud our view of Clare when she arrives.

Tim, as usual, arrives forty-five minutes early. We talk through various pointers regarding Peter and I prepare some lunch for us all, knowing that Clare will be here around midday, after a long drive. Only ten minutes later than scheduled, Clare arrives – and immediately she appears friendly and easy to talk to. Our first impression is a good one.

The meeting lasts about three hours altogether and it is a very, very different experience from the previous one. Clare talks animatedly about Peter, making him "come alive". She answers all of our questions and asks us many more, without ever making us feel that we are being unduly judged or interrogated. She seems to love our dogs, likes the house very much and she really seems to like us. She is very, very positive, even talking to Tim about arranging the next meeting to include the foster carer.

The only blot on the horizon is the fact that we are not the only family being considered for Peter after all. His details have been sent to another family who live only fifteen miles away from where he presently lives with his foster carer. Our hearts sink. Even though Clare seems extremely disinterested in visiting this other family, we know from experience that it is foolish to be too confident.

Nonetheless, when Clare asks if we would like to see Peter's life story book, we both say "yes". We have decided that we definitely want to see a picture of this little boy who might become our son, and the life story book turns out to be a revelation.

There is Peter's birth certificate, his first romper suit, first baby photos, pictures of birth mum and grandma, and letters from previous foster carers. It is a potted history of Peter's life and we feel privileged to be allowed to share in it. But it makes us think that if we do end up losing this child as well as Annie, then we might have to give up. Once you see photos of a child – a beaming face, a glimpse into their personality – you are deeply involved already.

Peter, seeing your shock of auburn hair and huge green eyes, you could so easily be our biological son. We so want to meet you, so want to have the chance to take care of you. And I do not know yet whether we will be given that chance. Robbie says to me later that evening, 'Clare must be pretty sure of us to show us Peter's life story work. Otherwise, it would be just too cruel a thing to do.'

Friday 1 August 2003

The very next day Tim rings to update us. He has heard from Clare, and she very much wants to proceed with Rob and me. As far as she is concerned, the other family lives too close to Peter's birth family and she thinks it is imperative that Peter lives some distance away from his home town.

Everything is looking very good indeed. Clare will run things past her manager the following Monday or Tuesday, and then we will have a final decision.

Who would have believed it? Only a couple of weeks earlier we were in the depths of despair. Our families, friends, and indeed our social worker, were all at a loss as to what to say to us.

And now just look at us!

But I have to say again just how hard the waiting becomes – and we have had to wait a short time compared to many other adopters we know. But only a matter of days can stretch into an agonising length of time. You try to keep busy and endeavour to fill your mind with something else, but it is quite impossible. Impossible when the decision could be life-changing.

Monday 4 August 2003

Tim rings us on the Monday afternoon to tell us that he hasn't heard anything yet. He himself is tense and says he cannot begin to imagine how Rob and I must be feeling.

We are like coiled springs, in fact. All our family and friends have been glued to their phones for the entire week, and the tension is mounting. My parents are almost tying themselves in knots with the anxiety, and desperately trying to remain positive. Rob's mum is almost too scared to ring – wanting to know while not wanting to bombard us with questions.

Wednesday 6 August 2003

Robbie and I are beginning to feel physically ill – we just cannot understand what is holding things up. Tim has spoken to Clare and she has assured him that everything is fine. She has decided not to assess the other family and wants to recommend only us. She tells us that she is merely waiting to have the "official" approval from her boss. Her manager is on leave and she has to apply to the Head of the Adoption Services to get the go ahead. This, it seems, is taking time.

Thursday 7 August 2003

Finally, at lunchtime, the phone call comes.

It is Tim; he congratulates us on becoming parents at last. Clare has emailed him to say that it has all been made official. She is delighted to tell us that Peter is to be our son!

On hearing the news I literally scream down the phone. Tim is happy for us both and is not in the least bit surprised when I start crying.

My friend, Janeen, is here when the news comes, having called round for lunch with her little boy. I am truly grateful that she is with me as I soon become quite emotional with the enormity of it all. For almost nine years Rob and I have waited for the moment when we can say that we are going to be parents. Now, at long last, that moment is here. For me it is like seeing the blue line on a pregnancy test for the very first time. Nothing else compares.

I phone Robbie at work and tell him the good news. He is overjoyed, of course, and comes home early and we start ringing round everyone we know.

We are particularly touched by the response of our nephew and niece, Luke and Bethany, aged nine and four. They have taken a great interest all the way along and have waited patiently for news, sometimes thinking that it was never going to happen! They are excited when we tell them that we are going to have a son. Especially Bethany when she realises that her new cousin will be so close to her in age. She asks whether Peter will be with us at Nana and Grandad's on Christmas Day. We take immense delight in saying, 'yes, we hope our little boy will definitely be part of the family by the time Christmas comes around'.

Congratulations and a multitude of gifts arrive from all and sundry. Rob's work colleagues astound me with their generosity. I swear we receive far more presents than we would have done if I'd just given birth to a baby!

Peter's foster carer is due to come down to see us next

Tuesday, along with Clare. They are going to bring some photos of Peter for us to keep, and at long last we will be able to show everyone what our son looks like. That will be a wonderful feeling.

As Tuesday approaches, Rob and I become more and more excited. We are especially keen to meet Peter's foster carer for, after all, she knows our son better than anyone else. Peter has lived with her family for over a year now, so it will be good to get a real feel for him from someone so close, as well as hearing all about his routines and his favourite things.

Tuesday 12 August 2003

Tim gets here early to see if there is anything we need to discuss before the meeting. He also runs through the list of questions we have prepared for the foster carer. When she arrives, we are delighted to find that she is such a warm, friendly, and easy person to talk to. This is such a relief, as we know that we will have to work closely with her in the future. Not only has she brought a whole stack of photos for us to look at and keep, but she has also brought a video, some of it filmed only the day before. The photos are fabulous – really expressive action shots and so many pictures of Peter laughing. He looks a happy little boy and has the most impish smile ever.

The video is wonderful. It really brings Peter alive for us, as we watch him running around with ducks on a recent holiday and playing with his toys at home. Seeing the video does feel surreal – watching our son-to-be talking into a camera only twenty-four hours before.

Robbie and I spend a long time chatting with Peter's foster carer. She couldn't be nicer and we can both really empathise with her. It is going to be tough for her to part with Peter.

It is arranged that a lot of Peter's belongings will be coming with him, like his stroller, car seat and bedding. It will help him to settle in and feel more comfortable, as otherwise, everything at our house will be new to him.

Rob and I are asked if we can make a video of ourselves, the dogs, our house and the town where we live. We are also asked to prepare a photo album that will be taken to Peter before he meets us, so that he can become familiar with our pictures.

We talk a lot about preparing for the introductions to Peter – pencilled in for late autumn – a few weeks after his third birthday. For the first week Robbie and I will be staying in Peter's home town, visiting him for an hour at first, then an afternoon, then getting him up first thing in the morning and so on until he trusts us enough to take him out on our own, prepare his tea and put him to bed. Then Rob and I will return home, collect the dogs from the kennels and continue with the introductions at our house. Peter will travel down with his foster carer and they will stay at a nearby hotel. Every meeting will be taken at Peter's pace. Nothing will be rushed or forced, and although the time span is pencilled in for two weeks, a lot of flexibility will be allowed. A review at our house, a week into the introductions, will help everyone to assess how things are going.

After the meeting we have great fun collecting together all the pictures of our family for the album. It feels strange to imagine our three-year-old son turning over the pages, seeing pictures of his new mummy and daddy for the first time. Very scary for him – such a leap into the unknown. It will be a similar leap into the unknown for us, of course, but at least we are adults and can make sense of what is happening. It will seem very confusing to a three-year-old. He will surely need masses of reassurance, love and patience – and so, for that matter, will we.

The next stage of the proceedings for us is to redesign Peter's bedroom in our house and to start buying all those extra bits and pieces such as stair gates, toy boxes, bedding and clothes.

Late August – September 2003

We have the best time ever, buying all and sundry for Peter's bedroom. We are hoping to recreate a look similar to his room in the foster carers' home. We choose bright blue wallpaper, Tweenies bedding, Winnie The Pooh pictures and masses of cuddly toys and books. We have to guess Peter's actual size from the photos, so choosing clothes is a bit of a gamble – and we know that some things will probably swamp him like a tent! It doesn't matter, these are absolutely magical weeks, as all of our hopes and dreams turn into reality.

We constantly email the foster carer (especially around Peter's third birthday, though it is hard not being able to join in the celebrations). This proves invaluable in helping us feel connected to what is happening at the other end of the country. Tim is also brilliant in phoning and keeping us up to date with what is going on.

One thing that is particularly painful to hear, however, is how upset Peter has become at the thought of moving away from the foster carers' home. This is entirely understandable and not unexpected, but it is still really distressing. Rob and I feel powerless to help, which of course we are. It certainly takes the shine off our sense of jubilation, and we just hope that things will start to get easier for Peter as time goes on.

Sure enough, Peter gradually becomes less upset at the prospect of moving although he is still rather bemused by the whole thing. Robbie and I send some recent photos of the dogs and us, as well as some postcards of our town and the nearby seaside. We also send a map, so that Peter will be able to understand where the "South of England" is exactly!

We then begin to put together our video for Peter. We spend many a day filming our dogs playing and we do our very best to try and convey our love and warmth through the lens of a camera. I so want our son to enjoy it.

It is harder than we imagine to pick out all the fun

things which might be of interest to a small child. Showing Peter his bedroom (with the aid of some hand puppets!) we hope will be a winner. We have spent so much time getting his bedroom right and we hope it will remind Peter of his present room – to make the transition from one home to another just that little bit easier.

As the weeks progress, heading towards our last but all-important panel, which will be asked to recommend our match with Peter, we go through another gamut of emotions, everything from fear to euphoria. It is an incredible time, and friends who have adopted say that they felt the same way.

After what seems an age, the weeks and days suddenly accelerate rather too quickly. Before we know it, we are only one week away from panel and introductions, and preparing for our last visit from our social worker, Tim. Neither of us can really believe that in seven days' time we will be meeting our son for the very first time.

Words cannot do justice to how we are feeling.

Monday 13 October 2003
The meeting with Tim goes well – he calms our nerves and shares our pleasure. He likes the bedroom and thinks that the album of family pictures is great.

We talk about the final preparations for panel in a couple of days. Neither of us has to attend which, quite frankly, we are rather glad about. Tim will be representing us and he will hand over the video and photo album to Clare, to take to the foster carer's house. Peter will then be able to look at them as many times as he wants, before we eventually arrive the following Tuesday.

Tim also talks us through our impending meeting with Peter's birth mother, which is taking place the day before we get to meet Peter. Both Rob and I have more misgivings and feel more apprehensive about this meeting than we have about anything else so far. Tim will also be present, as well as Clare, who will be supporting Peter's birth mother.

We keep reminding ourselves that we have agreed to this meeting for Peter's sake. We will get the chance to ask certain questions and it could be good for Peter's birth mother, hopefully, to come away from the meeting feeling a little more positive about the two people who will be raising her son. All very difficult, and I have a feeling that our meeting may get somewhat emotional.

I'll never forget these few days before we meet Peter. Our panel date passes without complications, apart from yet another reprimand about my smoking. We are now on the final countdown to what the adoption process has been about. Everything becomes a whirlwind of activity. We frantically buy the last few bits for the house and enjoy some time out for just the two of us. We fill the cupboards with child-friendly foods. Then, before we know it, it is the night before we are due to drive up north to our hotel – which will be our home for the next seven nights.

Sunday 19 October 2003

We are elated and feel physically sick. Morning is here and we are packing our suitcases into the car. It really is happening. We are about to meet our son and the next chapter of our life will begin.

Peter, I hope and pray that you will like your new mummy and daddy, and I promise you that we will do everything in our power to make you feel a safe and happy little boy.

9

And then there were three

OCTOBER–DECEMBER 2003

To our son

I dreamt of you last night, even though I have yet to meet you. I dreamt that I took your hand and held you with my love.

I know it will not be that easy – but this morning, when I woke, I also knew that no matter how hard it may be, your new mummy and daddy will always be there to look after you.

And to love you. Forever.

That is our pledge to you.

Tuesday 21 October 2003

I catch my breath as I glimpse our son standing at the foster carers' front door, a beaming smile etched upon his face, his hand waving madly.

It is 2pm on Tuesday afternoon and we are due to take Peter to the park with his foster carer. It will be a short meeting – a couple of hours; we are supposed to act as naturally as possible, while introducing ourselves as Peter's new mummy and daddy!

That first meeting is heaven – although no, you do not fall in love instantly, as any truthful adopter will tell you.

But we do feel a rush of affection towards this child. We also feel slightly awkward, anxious and anything but natural.

We have imagined this moment for years, and suddenly here we are, examining every single inch of our child's face.

We struggle to take it all in. Now we are parents. Perhaps this is akin to holding your newborn baby in your arms for that very first time. The moment will stay with me forever, of that I'm sure. It is one of those landmarks in our lives that we will re-live a thousand times over.

Wednesday 22 October 2003
We have a very early start, so that we can arrive before Peter wakes up.

This is when we both begin to feel quite alarmingly out of our depth – standing in someone else's house – watching whilst a family (with other foster children) goes about its daily routine. It is 6am, still dark outside, and we are not yet fully awake after an almost sleepless night.

To make matters worse, Peter is not in the best of moods when he wakes; he is confused as to why we are there and who we are. We see the first glimpses of an explosive temper.

We have been told about his tantrums, of course, but witnessing little fists flying is another thing entirely. Peter is finding the attention and disruption to his routine unsettling. We have been warned that this might be the case, and on this second day of introductions, the reality begins to hit home.

Thursday 23 October 2003
On the third morning, Robbie and I are expected to prepare Peter's breakfast, which fortunately he loves. Both of us still feel ill at ease in the foster carers' house; we also feel extremely sorry for them, having two strangers descend on them at six in the morning and take over. It feels horribly artificial and contributes to me having problems

assessing my true feelings about the whole adoption, coupled with the fact that I have a nasty chest infection and I am seriously sleep-deprived.

Being holed up in a noisy hotel for a week, away from family, friends and anything "familiar" is also hard. Both of us are feeling the strain and sensing an overall lack of support. The meeting we endured on arrival in Peter's home town was nothing short of awful. Every single moment of the two-week introduction was dissected in minute detail. Tensions and emotions were running high and not everyone around the table seemed to agree with all the finer details of the plan. The foster carers kept breaking down in tears and Clare was looking more and more annoyed. At the end of the meeting we were handed a stack of life story books and other documents and then left to make our way back to the hotel. Neither Tim nor Clare nor anyone seemed concerned about how we might be feeling. It was disappointing and the cracks were starting to show.

Thursday afternoon

One thing that does go remarkably well is the meeting with Peter's birth mother. This is pencilled in for this afternoon, and when the moment comes I am within an inch of saying that I can't go through with it. But in the end I do.

The meeting is delayed by two hours, so by the time we're taken to the social services department to meet Peter's birth mother, we are making ourselves ill with anxiety. We have been plied with so much discouraging information that it is fair to say that we are not at all keen to meet her.

Clare keeps reassuring us that it will be fine and that she 'knows how to handle Peter's mother'. Tim remains calm throughout. The meeting itself is fairly short and Peter's mother is as nice as could be. My heart goes out to her, and all I want to do is hug her. She seems so alone, and I feel guilty for wanting to become Peter's new mother. She is very young and immature and quiet throughout our exchange. At the end of the meeting we have our photo taken together, to be placed in one of Peter's numerous life story books.

We promise to maintain letterbox contact once a year, with photos included. No matter how much she may have neglected or failed Peter in the past, we feel she deserves this at least. We just hope that she will not get herself pregnant again, as Clare fears. For if she does, the whole sad cycle might be repeated, and she will lose another child.

Friday 24 – Sunday 26 October 2003

We gradually begin to enjoy more quality time alone with Peter, taking him out for the afternoon, feeding the ducks, taking photos, playing, having a hug and walking together. These moments are lovely.

Initially Peter has bonded with Robbie more quickly than with me, which hurts, so when he begins to call me "Mummy" and doesn't always turn to the foster carer instead of me, it is truly wonderful. Clearly, Peter is still finding introductions rather confusing, and is prone to some fairly knee-jerk tantrums. He will call me "mummy" when out, then call the foster carer "mum" when we return. It must be painfully hard for this little boy to even begin to know whom to turn to. My own emotions are certainly being pushed to their limits this week. And so are the foster carer's. This lady has the unenviable task of having to distance herself from a child who has been in her care for over a year. She tries to remain supportive and encouraging to us both, as do her husband and younger son.

Although we have a couple of successful outings to nature reserves and parks, as well as an award-winning tantrum in McDonalds, when Peter flings himself on the floor like a starfish, both Robbie and I are keen to be back on our own home turf. We really need to start feeling like a proper family and in control of the situation. Peter also seems eager to meet our two dogs; the foster carers have dogs, so it is something he is comfortable with. We are keen to collect them from the kennels and see how that first meeting will go.

Before we return down south, Clare and some fellow social workers join us at the foster family's house for a "pause and reflect" meeting. We tell Tim not to worry about making the three hour-long-journey; with hindsight, it would have been infinitely better if he had been present.

The meeting is excruciating – everyone firing questions at us, our emotions ragged by this point. I begin to feel threatened, and even start to doubt my own abilities to be a parent.

After much deliberation, it is decided to see how the introductions continue on our home territory. Our departure proves to be very traumatic for Peter, mainly because he sees us packing a lot of his toys and clothes into our jeep. This will be Peter's sixth move in three years and he becomes hysterical at the prospect, lashing out at the foster carer and screaming in sheer confusion. It is both heartbreaking and frightening to witness.

When we eventually arrive back home, it is fantastic to be on familiar ground again. I can't help feeling that perhaps we should have done this earlier.

We indicate to Tim and Clare that it would be good to have more time alone with Peter as we feel he needs to be given the clear message that Robbie and I are his new "permanent" mummy and daddy. They agree whole-heartedly – and so does the foster carer. Tea for everyone on Day 1 is reduced to tea for Peter, Robbie and myself.

Tuesday 28 October 2003

Peter does not seem unduly concerned by the foster carers leaving after they drop him at our house; he probably realises that he will see them later on. We have a good time together and Peter instantly bonds with our two dogs, who become his newest playmates. He loves his bedroom and even asks if he may stay the night with us, snuggled under his Tweenies duvet. We have to say 'no, not tonight' as he is not yet allowed to stay over. We make the most of the time available, playing with bubbles and playdoh and crayoning crazy pictures. Gleeful shouts of 'Mummy' as we prepare tea together simply make my heart melt.

Wednesday 29 – Friday 31 October 2003

We collect Peter every morning from the foster carers' rented cottage. Normally this produces a massive (and very distressing) tantrum, as he doesn't want to leave the foster carers' son. We sometimes have to physically restrain Peter in order to get him into the car seat; by the time we get back to our house, he has normally quietened down.

In general Peter's moods are very up and down – as you would expect from a muddled and insecure three-year-old. One minute he is playing games, squealing with delight, and the next he is screaming in our faces and kicking at the dogs. We are very aware that most of this behaviour is due to his circumstances. Some of it is simply down to the fact that Peter is a normal, boisterous and very strong-willed three-year-old boy!

In the middle of this second week, we have another review to see how things are going. Clare and Tim come to our house and watch us playing together. Peter is in a good mood and eats his lunch beautifully at the table. We all play with his bubble gun and do masses of jigsaws. Both social workers seem pleased, and Rob and I are feeling much happier and more confident. It is decided that Peter will move in with us for good in two days' time. The foster carers will come in for a quick cup of tea, some last minute photos, and then they will leave for their return journey home.

It has also been decided that we will not go back north to say our goodbyes; it had seemed a bad idea to us in the first place to drag Peter back to the foster carers' house, just to say goodbye. It is too long a journey to go there and back in one day – and everyone is of the opinion that Peter will become even more confused if he goes back to his previous home, only to be wrenched away again. He is already upset each time we pick him up from the holiday cottage. So, on the last two days of introductions the foster carers will drop Peter off at our house instead. This seems to work a whole lot better. Things really start to improve on our last two outings with Peter, although Clare feels that an overnight stay would not be a good idea. She thinks we should wait until he moves in with us for good. We now feel prepared for that moment, even though we still have to pinch ourselves to believe that it's really happening.

Saturday 1 November 2003
I cannot convey how Rob and I feel when we wake in the morning and realise that our son moves in with us today.

It will be our last "lie-in" (until 7am – Peter normally wakes at about five!).

It will be our last few moments together as a couple.

It will be my last morning yearning to be a mum.

We will finally be a family, we will finally have our son.

Robbie and I are awed by the immensity of what we are taking on. The foster carers have been extremely supportive over the last few days, but everyone's emotions are just about wrung dry. There have been times when I've wanted to crawl under the duvet and fast forward six months, just to see how we have settled down. The constant pressure on us as a couple is relentless and unforgiving. We are lucky in that we have such a strong relationship to support one another, Robbie is especially caring as my health is beginning to suffer. In the first week of introductions I lost three-quarters of a stone in weight. It has undoubtedly been a testing two weeks.

In our workshops, some eighteen months ago now, we were warned that introductions would be physically and emotionally exhausting. We were also told that any seemingly dormant feelings regarding infertility might rear their ugly head again – and yes, they did. But neither Robbie nor I feel that we were prepared enough for the strain of a long distance adoption, especially that of a three-year-old, whose capacity to understand what was going on must have been next to nothing. If *I* can hardly describe how tough the last two weeks have been, then for a vulnerable little boy it must have been hell.

The morning passes in a blur. The foster carers arrive at nine, stay for tea and photos and leave quietly and without any fuss, their emotions bravely concealed from Peter. Peter is fairly nonchalant about their leaving, but then we knew he would be, as he couldn't possibly comprehend that they are going back to their home without him.

The day goes well; it is somewhat strange perhaps, but immense fun when we visit a nearby nature centre. Rob and I try hard to pick up on Peter's feelings. He likes his dinner, as well as his bath; his bedtime story is followed by a surprisingly easy drift off to sleep.

As Rob and I enjoy a celebratory glass of wine downstairs, we are like rabbits caught in headlamps – the television barely audible and talking in no more than a whisper. It is quite comical really, especially when we venture to bed, hardly daring to breathe in case we wake our gorgeous new son.

Sunday 2 November 2003
Peter wakes early, at about 4.30am to be precise! To his credit we manage to persuade him to go back to bed for another half hour or so, with the promise of a lovely breakfast and a story when we all get up.

Mid-morning we all walk the dogs together. One minute Peter is helping to hold the leads and then he is suddenly sitting on the pavement looking thoughtful and is reluctant to move.

Later, we embark on our weekly shop, something that a lot of our friends with children think is very brave. Amazingly, Peter is quite content, his independent streak shining through as he insists on helping to put everything in the trolley for us.

In the afternoon, far too soon in retrospect, we stop off at my parents, so that Peter can meet them. He is reluctant to go in at first, so my mother comes out with a present and some chocolate buttons, which soon seem to do the trick!

The visit goes well; we stay about an hour. Peter is happy and enjoys playing with the cars and toy animals on offer, while both my parents simply ooze love and affection for their newest grandson. He does, however, seem confused as to where his "bedroom" is in this house. We realise that the visit has made him unsure where he is sleeping tonight.

When we return home, Peter's behaviour becomes increasingly aggressive and defiant – going to Nana and Grandad's house has thrown him. He becomes so difficult to placate that we quickly realise that any future meetings with family and friends would have to be on neutral territory, such as a park, or at our house.

The next four weeks
Over the next couple of weeks we meet up with Robbie's mum, who by now is impatient to meet her grandchild. We choose a park this time, and for the most part the meeting goes well. We also get together at our house with my brother, his wife and my nephew and niece. Peter seems very taken with Luke and Bethany. They play wonderfully together and it is a joy to see.

Equally, Peter enjoys meeting our closest friends when they visit, and naturally he loves all the attention and the numerous gifts.

His behaviour is as changeable as the wind and, although somewhat expected, it still has the power to shock. There is one particular day when he wakes in a terrible mood and the day spirals downhill from there. There are too many tantrums to count (well, we do count at least seven, each lasting up to an hour). There is kicking, crying, punching, and absolutely no reasoning with Peter at all. Another day there is breath-holding; another day an attempt to throw himself headfirst down the stairs. He can take delight in hurting the dogs and hurting us.

Rob and I sometimes feel that we have been "thrown to the lions". We knew about some of Peter's aggressive behaviour, but living with it is different. Still, it doesn't detract from the fact that seventy per cent of the time Peter is the most adorable, charming, stubborn but delightfully bright little boy who is also angry and confused by his past. He is angry with the foster carers' son for leaving him, so we quickly send off a letter and some photos. The foster carers' son writes back to explain his departure to Peter – and this does help to settle him a little.

Tim, our social worker, tries to be as supportive as he can. He listens to me crying down the phone on more than one occasion and comes to visit Robbie and me in the evening, so that we can talk openly. He wonders whether play therapy might help Peter. His play is very aggressive – he strangles his toys and attacks any "friends" amongst them. To be brutally honest, in the first couple of weeks we had moments of doubt, and even close family and friends couldn't quite understand how upsetting it could be to see a three-year-old in so much distress.

Things start to improve little by little. Eating and toileting become less of a control issue for Peter as he learns to feel more secure. He has always called us "mummy" and "daddy", but now there are hugs, face-stroking and kisses. We begin to recognise the triggers for his tantrums, and to feel a little more in charge.

It seems that all those people who told us life would never be the same again were right! The responsibility for another human being, especially one so needy and deserving of so much love, is scary. Suddenly, not a second of the day is our own any more; we do not even have the privacy of a closed toilet door (well, not unless our foot is holding it, that is!). I'm sure any parent of any toddler in the land will say the same. Listening to my friends with even younger children, I sometimes think we are getting off lightly!

So life goes on, marked by a series of visits from social workers who come pretty much every week at first to "observe" how Peter is doing.

These visits are invariably fairly uncomfortable and something that I do not look forward to. Obviously the "looked after child" has to be monitored regularly, but we very much feel reminded that Peter is still legally the responsibility of a local authority in the north of England. Indeed, at the four-week review – a very formal meeting at our house with a chairperson – Robbie and I are left in no doubt as to where we stand.

Thursday 27 November 2003

Although we are praised for the improvement in Peter's behaviour, social services decide to effectively undo all our hard work to make Peter feel secure, by sending us to meet up with the foster carers again within the next few weeks.

We are left reeling. We had previously agreed to meet the foster carers again the following summer. This suited them very well, bearing in mind that they have not only their own children to consider but also their foster children, and it also suited us. We had all been very happy with this arrangement.

However, according to Clare, it would be better for Peter to bring this contact meeting forward by at least six months, to before Christmas, or at least the very beginning of January 2004.

We, as Peter's parents, feel that this is far too soon, and that not only will it unsettle Peter and shake his new-found stability, it might also bring back his feelings of anger and aggression. We are told that yes, that may well happen, but it is something social services feel should be done now so that, quote, 'Peter can at least see that they're not dead'.

Tim agrees that Clare is exercising control in a way that

is hard for us to deal with. The foster carer almost falls out with Clare saying that Rob and I should have much more say in the matter, as we are now Peter's parents.

That is the very crux of the matter. We are left with barely veiled threats about 'having to be sure about the placement', which tells us that until an Adoption Order is made by the court, we have no legal responsibility for Peter at all. So we have to say 'yes' to whatever is planned for us.

We do not believe that our own – or our son's – feelings come into the equation. Peter is fine about knowing where the foster carers are and we have already exchanged letters and photos with them. We feel that it will disturb him greatly to travel up north to meet them again so soon.

Social workers see things differently, so that is the end of the matter – and life does go on.

On a more positive note, it is the build-up to Christmas.

December 2003

Our first Christmas together. Not only are Rob and I excited, but also family, friends and even people we barely know, reach out to wish us well, and the presents for Peter start arriving by the sackful!

Sometimes people's generosity is too much; you can end up feeling like a bit of an exhibit, and the child can become somewhat overwhelmed by all the fuss! But most of the time people's interest and joy for us as a family is heartfelt and genuine.

The build-up to Christmas is an unforgettable time for many reasons. Peter is naturally bemused by it all but he knows that something very special is happening. Rob and I – having had some stressful moments to deal with – at last feel the knot in our stomachs unravelling a little. Family and friends, and social workers too, are amazed at how things have steadily improved after a difficult start.

More important than any of that for me is how I feel myself changing towards Peter on an almost daily basis. Any fear that this is not right for us has all but gone. I know that I am falling deeply in love with our son, and Robbie feels exactly the same way. I have wondered how long it will take before I say 'I love you' to Peter at night and truly mean it.

Well, only a few days before Christmas I mean it – and I no longer see his birth mother's face staring back at me every time I gaze into his beautiful green eyes. Instead, I see his love for us shining back, which is a quite wonderful and defining moment.

Robbie and I are so looking forward to the future, and looking forward to our first Christmas together as a family. We are looking forward to seeing in the New Year with our wonderful son. A New Year of challenges and surprises and a bond growing ever deeper.

10

Expect the unexpected

DECEMBER 2003–JUNE 2004

For many years Rob and I simply accepted the fact that Christmas was always going to be a very difficult time for us – a time for children and therefore a time when our childlessness was all the more apparent, and ever more painful.

So it was with joyful abandon that we threw ourselves into the Christmas of 2003. Not since I was a child had I been so excited, and so apprehensive too. Rob and I just hoped and prayed that Peter would enjoy his first Christmas with us as a family although we had no idea how things might turn out.

Wednesday 25 December 2003
Christmas Day finally arrives. It seems quite unreal when our three-year-old son gleefully grabs the stocking from the end of his bed, with us barely believing that WE are his parents!

We capture the moment on film; it is priceless. Peter is thrilled by all his presents, though still somewhat awe-struck and mixed up about the whole Father Christmas thing. He doesn't really understand what Christmas Day means – and we wouldn't expect him to. We know this moment is more for us to cherish than for Peter. It is the moment we have only dared to dream about, and now it is ours to enjoy.

Peter is particularly keen to give the dogs their presents. We notice that he delights in seeing which presents we have all received. He really wants to be part of the bigger picture. He is not in the least a self-centred little boy.

We have lunch at Rob's mum's house, with his younger sister Susie. It goes remarkably well, better than we dared expect, especially as Peter can still be very unpredictable in other people's houses: sullen and withdrawn one minute and screaming and crying the next. He seems surprisingly content and we have a most relaxing afternoon.

Boxing Day is a similar success, spent at my parents, with my brother, his wife and our nephew and niece. Peter can't wait to play with them. Again, he is in great form, with only minor upsets once or twice – absolutely nothing that you wouldn't get from any over-excited three-year-old. Christmas could evoke very mixed memories for Peter; if it does, he manages to hide his feelings remarkably well and is absorbed in his play.

I cannot help but wonder what sort of Christmas Peter's birth mother is having. I cannot help but wonder how the foster carers are coping – thinking back to their last Christmas, which will have been so very different.

I'd be lying if I said that I feel completely OK with everything. I find myself very emotional at times; no matter how much I am growing to love Peter, things are still not as easy as I'd rather naively hoped. He does, after all, come with a huge amount of emotional baggage – something we have read about, but witnessing it on a regular basis is upsetting, and we often feel powerless to help.

How I wish I could have shared in Peter's first three years.

How I wish I could erase the bad memories from his mind.

How I wish that Peter hadn't suffered as he has. I know

it is pointless going down this particular road; it causes nothing but heartache. We know that we are so lucky to have Peter, and we intend to make the most of every minute of our time together. It was meant to be. We are proud to have such an enchanting little boy to call our son. He is enormous fun – and enormously hard work too! We really begin to wonder about our lives before Peter came to live with us; I mean, what did we do with ourselves half of the time?

We do still try to make some time for just the two of us. That first trip to a restaurant as a couple, after Peter came to live with us, was quite blissful. It gave us time to recharge the batteries – we should never underestimate the impact of a young child on one's love life – or sanity!

January 2004
After seeing in the New Year, we are thrust headfirst into 2004, and the day that I've been dreading suddenly looms ever closer.

It is the day when we are due to go and meet the foster carers again. To me it is the day our little boy is being put to the test. Rob and I still view it as such an ill-timed meeting. We are so worried that it will set us back a pace, at a time when we have all made such great strides forward.

We decide to meet the foster carers at a safari park – half-way between our two homes. It is a bitterly cold day and it soon starts to snow. This is a good thing, as Peter is enthralled by the falling snowflakes.

In the event, the meeting goes surprisingly well – especially from our perspective. Peter acts exactly as Tim, our social worker, has predicted. He is quiet, shy and unforthcoming for the first twenty minutes. He clings to Rob and me and, although friendly to the foster carers, is uncharacteristically subdued and cautious. He doesn't understand what the meeting is about. His attachment to us is unquestionable.

I am selfishly overjoyed to see this with my own eyes,

even while I realise how tough it must be for the foster carers, who remain fantastic throughout. After a while Peter relaxes, finds his feet, and becomes much more his "old" self – noisy and full of energy, frantically chasing the foster carers' son.

I do not feel as threatened as I thought I would; I am more secure in my role as mum than I imagined. I am pleased that he has been able to see his young friend again and I am glad that the foster carers have had the opportunity to see for themselves how well Peter is doing.

The meeting lasts about ninety minutes – quite long enough, in such bitterly cold weather. The foster carers are amazed at how much Peter has changed both physically and emotionally. He seems so much more confident than they remember him. They admit how nervous they have been before the meeting and feel that Peter's response has been absolutely right for everyone concerned. They say that it will now enable them to move on, knowing their job is done. They gave Peter unconditional love and support at a crucial time in his life. To walk away from that to start again with another child must be unbelievably hard. I know I couldn't do it – I don't think many people can. They are special people, that's for sure, and we will always be grateful for the care they have given our son.

We part with an easy and natural "goodbye", no tears or tantrums. Peter is happy to get back in our car, knowing that we will meet up again in the summer. We exchange follow-up letters and photos.

Although Peter mentions the foster carers' young son a few times during the next couple of days, there is nothing like the backlash or reaction we feared.

Well, not for almost two weeks.

Tim is surprised by the delay. Clare seems a little oblivious of the effect it has upon us, as a family, to see our young son unravel – testing boundaries one minute, and clinging to us the next. He constantly wants to look through his life story work and bombards us daily with questions about the foster carers' son. He doesn't understand why he has disappeared again. We really feel for Peter who is clearly struggling to make sense of his world with only the vocabulary and understanding of a three-year-old.

Control issues surface once again, especially about toileting. This problem had all but disappeared before the contact meeting and now becomes a massive challenge all over again. We don't know how long it will take to get back on track. It is distressing both for Peter and for us.

For a couple of weeks Peter also becomes very tearful over the least thing. He begins strangling his toys again and taking one toy away from the others so that 'it has no friends'. His play generally shows frustrated aggression. He turns physically abusive within the blink of an eyelid and often kicks at us or bites or spits. His colourful drawings revert to heavy-handed black crayoning. It is heartbreaking to see. Basically his bedrock of security has been shaken, and it will take more time, love and patience before Peter regains his exuberance.

February 2004

When he does, it is fabulous. Suddenly we realise that he has not mentioned the foster carers' son for two to three weeks. He is happier, more co-operative and confident. His manners are a credit to him and his affection for others is noticeable. His play returns to normal for any boy of his age. His aggression slowly subsides and he is altogether more relaxed and at ease.

With hindsight we realise that the meeting with the foster carers would have proved stressful even if it had taken place in the summer, as planned. Perhaps as a family we needed to go through this challenge in order for Peter to come out the other side, reassured that he has not been forgotten. We are delighted, especially as Peter is due to start nursery shortly and we obviously want him to feel as secure and happy as possible beforehand. We have been encouraged by the foster carers and by Clare to enrol Peter at nursery as soon as possible, as this was part of his previous familiar routine. It will also be a good way for Peter to socialise regularly with children his own age as he needs to learn how to share with others.

When the day arrives, Peter is unfazed and looking forward to the prospect. I think because he liked nursery in his home town, he has a very positive attitude. However, Rob and I know that his behaviour in the previous nursery was somewhat challenging towards the other children and staff. He had already been excluded from one playgroup. Biting seemed to be the main trouble, so we are anxiously waiting to see whether these old behavioural patterns will re-emerge.

It seems we needn't have worried. On the very first day Peter is comfortable with being left for half an hour; we have prepared him in advance that I will be coming back very soon. There are the usual "learning to share" difficulties, but otherwise he is fine and I get a huge hug on my return. Peter seems delighted that he will soon be coming twice a week.

Rob and I are especially pleased with the nursery staff's attitude to adoption, as well as their tight security and their discretion when discussing our son. They have dealt with numerous adopted children before, and are amazed how quickly Peter seems happy at being left. They say that it's obvious he feels secure, and they tell me that other adopted children (and birth children too) have taken months to feel as safe as he does.

So nursery soon becomes a part of our routine and for three-and-a-half hours twice a week I have my old life back, though I can never fully "switch off" from wondering how Peter is getting on.

It is a peculiar feeling at first. All my friends with children say to me, 'Isn't it great to have some time to yourself?' And I reply, 'Yes, but I miss him,' and wonder whether I'm allowed to have this "guilt free" time anymore.

I do believe that nursery is great for children – it is great for Peter – and I know that it is good for me too. I can do shopping, housework or indeed write this diary without interruptions every two minutes!

Life is good and Peter seems content. He is now far more easy about going to other people's houses because he knows we will always come home again. He is loving and desperate to help with chores around the house, but he can also entertain himself.

Rob and I cannot believe that Peter has only been with us for three-and-a-half months. The change in him is astonishing; anger and aggression are giving way to trust. We can only hope that as Peter gets older his temperament will remain on this even keel. Time will tell on that one.

Friday 27 February 2004

It is now almost four months since the initial placement – and we are getting ready for the next big review with social workers and health visitors at our house. This time everyone will decide whether we can go ahead and apply to court for an Adoption Order.

We are relieved that the answer is a unanimous 'yes'. Everyone seems happy with the progress we are making as a family. Clare, who started out with so much enthusiasm and vigour, now seems keen to move on from the case, and says as much to Rob and me. We can understand her feelings up to a point. Peter has been under her care for a very long time now and she wants to see a permanent happy conclusion. But she makes us feel that everything to do with us has become a bit of a chore. Maybe the long car journeys are beginning to take their toll. Certainly the sooner we go to court, the better.

Tim remains as supportive as ever – so does our health visitor. Everyone at the meeting is keen to get the papers completed and signed. The court hearing will be nearby, so that we won't have to travel hundreds of miles to Peter's home town. We are really pleased at this news – it would have been a horrendously long day for Peter otherwise.

March – end April 2004
As the weeks and months roll on towards a court date, we begin to take stock of all the "firsts" we are experiencing as parents.

We take Peter swimming – which he takes to at once, showing no fear and a capacity for quick learning in the pool.

We take him on a double-decker bus and we take him on the train – the tunnels are greeted with whoops of delight!

We start going out for the occasional Sunday lunch, and Peter seems to love family outings and is remarkably well behaved.

We book our first holiday together to a farm in the West Country. Peter knows that he will be able to help milk the cows, as well as feed the lambs and collect the eggs. I swear he runs around the room screaming with joy for at least five minutes when we tell him!

Mother's Day is another special landmark – my first homemade Mother's Day card becomes one of my most prized possessions.

Life is suddenly quite lovely and quite "normal". We almost start to feel like an ordinary family in the neighbourhood. Which is why it can become seriously annoying that often well-meaning neighbours, some of whom I have barely spoken to before, keep commenting on the adoption. Do they not realise that a boy of Peter's age can comprehend a lot of what is being said? As a close friend observes, when you adopt a child you seem to become "public property". First there are questions and assumptions regarding your infertility, and then very personal questions about your child's history and background. 'So where did he come from then?' left me incredulous. Just as infuriating was 'When do you think you'll adopt another?' as if everything in life were that simple and as if we'd picked Peter off a shelf. I have to remind myself that, for a lot of people, adoption is a bit of a mystery, something that is much talked about, but little is known about. Therefore, it is understandable that people are curious to find out more.

Misguided neighbourly enquiries, as well as visits from Clare, affect Peter for some time afterwards, especially since he has become more aware of references to the adoption hearing. And he still associates Clare with all his traumatic moves in the past.

It is fair to say that we long for the day when we can shut our front door, have no more intrusions, and just get on with our lives like any other family. That will be so nice.

May 2004

Our elusive court date seems to be stretching further and further into the distance, even though we filed our application during the first week of March. This delay is due in part to Clare deciding that she isn't happy with the contact arrangements after all.

It has been agreed that Rob and I will write to his birth mother once a year, as we promised to do when we met her many months ago. It was deemed inappropriate for Peter to have contact with his grandma because of her erratic mental health and questionable care of Peter. This was given as one of the primary reasons for Peter to move to a different part of the country in the first place. His reticence when looking at photos of his grandma and birth mother speak volumes to us about how he has been treated.

Clare, however, has changed her mind and favours us writing to grandma once a year as well, although she has strong opinions about this lady, and none of them favourable. Her proposal will apparently have to be endorsed by the panel. Robbie and I are more than a little surprised and displeased. Clare reasons that, if Peter's birth mother does not maintain her letterbox contact, then grandma would provide a "back-up" so that Peter will receive at least one letter a year.

Once again, our opinion as adoptive parents is disregarded. We do not think that this plan will benefit Peter in the long run: grandma has been refused permission to see him since he was very young, and yet Peter is still haunted by memories of her.

At one point I say to Clare, 'If this letterbox contact upsets Peter in the future, what shall we do?'

Her response?

'Stop writing then' – simple as that.

So for the sake of this quite baffling decision on the social worker's part, everything is to be delayed by a further two to three months. It is now almost the end of May – and our review meeting was in February, when it was agreed that we should proceed as quickly as possible! Peter will have been living with us for almost a year before the adoption becomes official. We will still have social workers visiting us every few weeks, which unsettles Peter every time. The whole process is frustratingly long. I think this may well be a contributory factor when placements disrupt before the final Adoption Order is made.

June 2004

Our holiday in the West Country – staying on a working farm – is altogether wonderful; gloriously hot June weather, fabulous beaches, and baby lambs to feed with bottles of milk early every morning. We have the time of our lives – rock pooling for crabs, feeding chickens and pigs, and enjoying the best clotted cream scones that money can buy! We have never seen our son so happy and carefree as he is that week. Undoubtedly hard work at times, Peter is also delightfully inquisitive, enthusiastic and immense fun – he is our "icing on the cake", as we like to call it.

It is always a wrench when Rob has to go back to work after a weekend together. After our holiday on the farm it is an even bigger shock for Peter when life returns to normal. To his credit, he adapts quicker than we anticipated. It seems that as much as Peter would like us to be at home together all of the time, he realises that this is just not possible.

We still have to be fairly strict with Peter about some things, but he seems to thrive on firm boundaries, as well as, of course, on praise when he's been good. Sure, he can have his moods and tantrums like all three-year-olds, and his nursery school has encountered a few of those over the past few weeks! If Peter doesn't feel like playing with the other children, then nothing in the world is going to persuade him, and he is best left to his own devices. I'm sure that I was similar when I first started at nursery school. Like Peter, I had my own select group of friends, but also enjoyed playing on my own – so it would seem that my son and I have quite a lot in common!

Although still unpredictable at nursery, Peter has so many lovely qualities – his manners, his charm and the smile of an angel. He is so easy to love – and we love him.

It is not only we, his parents, who love Peter. Our family has embraced Peter from the very first moment they saw him. My mother and father have played an important role in making Peter feel secure, as has Rob's mum. Both my parents are retired and have the luxury of being able to see their grandson whenever they wish. My mother worked in a primary school for over twenty years, and has a natural understanding of young children. My dad was quite a strict father when Mark and I were growing up. To see him playing with Peter now, one would never believe it. He has our son in fits of laughter more than anyone I know! Peter clearly adores them both. He is comfortable spending time alone with either set of grandparents although he is still not at the stage where he could stay the night away from home. My mum in particular is looking forward to that moment and so are we. We will know when Peter is ready to take that next step.

We do feel very blessed to have such a close knit and supportive family surrounding us, sharing in our journey to adoption, which will soon be at an end.

How we long for that day to be here, though we know by now that the "waiting game" is such a big part of adoption. When you choose to adopt you have to learn to have patience, the hard way sometimes. We know that every day we are one step closer, and we just have to bide our time until that all important court date is upon us.

11

The waiting game

JULY–SEPTEMBER 2004

Peter has now been living with us for eight months. His speech has much improved and he has grown, not only in confidence, but also in stature. A fairly slight child, he is now a good two inches taller and almost half a stone heavier. He is very proud that he is getting to be a "big boy", often striking a pose to show us his muscles! We are so pleased for him – no one wants to be the smallest.

July 2004

After our glorious West Country holiday, Peter goes back to nursery school with enthusiasm – so much so that we decide to increase his sessions to three times a week. Peter has become more involved and he is regularly praised for his singing (something he had steadfastly refused to do for the first couple of months), as well as his dancing and painting. He is gradually warming to the other children and now mentions some of his "friends" by name. He is still having the occasional spectacular tantrum over "sharing" things, so Robbie and I try hard not to spoil Peter too much – though it is difficult not to indulge a child for whom you have waited almost a decade.

At the nursery Parents' Evening, "sharing" is the main

concern. The staff are used to dealing with this problem, and are aware that Peter has had to leave many possessions behind in the past. They take our advice to remain consistently firm with him. He is a bright little boy and responds to having things explained to him, and usually manages to change his behaviour accordingly. In time we are sure that he'll learn to share with others.

As Peter is our only child, people often ask us whether we would go through another adoption to have a brother or sister for Peter.

At the start of the whole process, the answer would have been 'yes'. Yes, we had assumed then that we would eventually adopt two children – perhaps a boy and a girl – and yes, we had planned ahead the way people often do. To have another child even half as lovely as Peter would be a stroke of good fortune. But two-and-a-half years later, Robbie and I can't see ourselves enduring the whole adoption business again. Apart from a reduced workshop at the very beginning, it would be pretty much the same the second time around.

All the intrusion again; all the self-doubts and anxious moments. All those questions we would have to ask ourselves again and again.

Will I get through the medical?

Will I be turned down for smoking? (Yes, most likely.)

Will Peter mind being questioned about a forthcoming brother or sister? (Yes, perhaps.)

Will he wonder why there are always social workers in our home? (Yes, definitely.)

It would not be fair on Peter. It could undo all of his newfound security, and that is a risk we are not prepared to take.

Also, I have to say that I simply could not cope with social workers "assessing" us again for the next couple of years. Somehow your life never feels your own. And the pain and uncertainty along the way can, at times, be unbearable. Emotional strength obviously differs from person to person but if, like me, you are prone to welling up at the least thing, then adoption on top of infertility can be pretty hard going.

Once was enough, thank you very much. Any grief that I once felt about my infertility has long since disappeared. I now regard myself the same as any other mother. We do not "crave" to have other children. Peter is everything we could ask for – and more.

The only time our feelings might change is if we one day receive a call from Peter's local authority to say that his biological mother has given birth again, and that the baby is free for adoption. Rob and I would have to think seriously about whether we could refuse Peter's blood brother or sister – assuming we were even offered the child and passed the next assessment. I cannot truthfully say now what Rob and I would do in such a situation. However, I sincerely hope that the scenario does not happen in the first place. Having met Peter's birth mother, I would not wish that heartache upon her all over again.

Late July – August 2004

Like a bolt from the blue, Peter appears to regress into some of his old behavioural patterns again: he is being defiant and extremely angry a lot of the time.

It is something of a shock and it takes us back to a place we have not been to in months. Something has clearly triggered an extreme response. We have tears and tantrums over the least thing, with Peter constantly challenging us, as well as seeming terribly sad.

Everything has run so smoothly lately, that we almost forgot that our child has come with enormous emotional baggage. As Tim points out, whereas these episodes happened all the time at first – then every few days, then every couple of weeks – now they just appear on the odd occasion. Even so, the severity of mood swings sends me reeling and more than once I am reduced to floods of tears.

But the gratifying thing about Peter is his ability to

realise when his behaviour has gone over the top. After repeatedly hitting a child in the park, he knows we need to talk. Out come the life story books and for more than an hour we pore over the photos. Peter can now verbalise so much more about what is going on. It turns out that he is missing the foster carers' son; a family event at the weekend has reminded him of a former outing.

He wonders why the foster carers' son can't come and live with us too – so that the two of them could play together in his bedroom. It breaks my heart to have to explain that he would not be able to come as he lives at home with HIS mummy and daddy – and they would miss him too much if he moved away.

Peter seems to understand, and together we write a letter to send to the foster carers' son along with some holiday photos. This makes Peter feel a whole lot better. When the foster carers' son replies with a letter and a colourful drawing, Peter is delighted. He knows that he is remembered.

During this stressful time with Peter, we finally receive the long awaited court papers from his social worker. There are three copies of a report about Peter and us, which have to be checked and signed. There is a lengthy Statement of Facts concerning birth family history and the reasons for dispensing with the birth mother's consent to the adoption. It is apparently common for birth parents to withhold their consent even if they have met the adopters and like them. The judge then has to rule whether consent is "being unreasonably withheld", and we are led to believe that this will be more or less a formality. I can understand mum not wanting to "sign him away", whatever the circumstances. I would feel the same in her place. Also included in the packet are details of the Care Order, when a Judge first ruled that Peter must be placed in the care of his local authority, and a cheque for the court costs.

Everything is pretty straightforward and nowhere near as complicated as we'd originally thought. Robbie and I duly sign the papers and photocopy everything for our own records. Then we run through it all with Tim, to make sure we haven't left anything out. Tim also helps us draft a letter to the court; the initial hearing for Peter's birth mother and the application to dispense with her consent is to be held in her home town. Rob and I have no say in this matter – it is the policy of this particular local authority. The final hearing, which we will have to attend with Peter, can be in a court near where we live.

Now we have to wait again.

Eventually we receive confirmation that our adoption application has at last been registered with the court. The letter explains the "directions of the Judge" in regard to the further conduct of the case before the matter can proceed. Tim reassures us that this is perfectly normal procedure. We are also informed that a Guardian *ad litem*, someone working for the court and completely independent of the case, will be visiting us, Peter's birth family, and the social workers.

I am not looking forward to this…yet another intrusive visit to our house. I'm afraid it will throw Peter off balance for a few days afterwards. The visit is necessary but we don't relish the thought of it.

Another thing that unsettles us further is the announcement that Tim, our social worker for the past eighteen months, is leaving his job. We are disappointed that he will not be at the final court hearing with us but we are also delighted for him; he has a promotion elsewhere, so who can blame him for going? Nonetheless, we are upset that we have to be allocated to a different social worker for the last, crucial few months. This will mean yet another new face for Peter to meet and wonder about: 'who are they and why are they are visiting our home?'

All of this is to be discussed at our next six-monthly review, a review we'd been told we probably wouldn't need, as we should have been to court by then.

Monday 16 August 2004

We have to exchange our first contact letters at this review meeting – one to the birth mother (including two photos) – and one to grandma, as we have been asked (well, told) to do. It soon transpires that the whole three-month delay, whilst we waited for panel to agree that we should write to grandma, has been for nothing. Nothing at all.

Grandma does not write a letter. Not one word – of which we are secretly very glad. However, birth mum does; a short but very nice letter – and sends a photo too.

Clare seems a touch embarrassed by the whole thing. She sincerely believed that the birth mother would not write – and that grandma would. It seems she was wrong.

We are so glad for Peter that this first year especially, his birth mother has made contact. We will not show him the letter until he is capable of more mature understanding, but it is touching that she has written to say that she hopes Peter is happy in his new home and is keeping well.

Our contact letter is not nearly as difficult to write as I had imagined. I'd wondered whether I might feel at all resentful or even jealous at having to inform Peter's birth mother of his progress. But I feel only sadness for her and find it easy to communicate how well Peter is doing. The reality is that I do not feel threatened by her in the least. Peter is our son now and, on a practical level, his birth family do not even know where we are living.

I realise only too well that as Peter grows up I may start to feel more insecure if he keeps on asking about his birth family. I hope we will be supportive if one day Peter chooses to trace his roots, and wishes to contact his birth mother. After all, it would be entirely natural for him to want to know about his start in life. If I had been adopted, then I'm sure I would burn with curiosity, and this would have no bearing on my love for the parents who'd brought me up. For now, this remains a bridge we might have to cross in the future.

September 2004

Two weeks after the review we receive a court date for the dispensation hearing in six weeks' time.

This is the big one. Because the birth mother is refusing to sign the adoption papers, the Judge needs to dispense with her consent for the adoption to proceed. It is what Robbie and I have been waiting for – and it is making us feel very nervous. In our hearts we know that everything will be fine, but at the same time we cannot wait to be given that final "seal of approval".

We are informed that the Guardian *ad litem* (now called Children's Guardian) will visit in the next few weeks. Apparently it is usual for him to go through the child's life story work. This is partly to check that the social worker has done his or her job properly, and partly to see that the adopters have continued with the good work.

We make it clear that in the light of a few recent nasty nightmares regarding people from his past, it would upset Peter to be reminded of painful events by a relative stranger. The Guardian agrees and will look at the early books without Peter. We do suggest that Peter would love to show him the life story albums we have made as a family, as he is immensely proud of them. Peter loves looking at all the photos of our family, dogs, holidays, friends and days out together. He always puffs out his chest with pride and beams from ear to ear when showing his favourite snaps. It is a joy to see.

During the weeks leading up to the first court date, Tim says farewell and we are introduced to our new social worker, Linda. She is a pleasant woman though quite dissimilar to Tim. At our last meeting, Peter gives Tim the most beautiful card, which he has spent a long time making, with paint and glitter and lots of sparkly stars. Inside, he has pasted a favourite photo of himself playing football in the garden. Tim looks very moved.

Clare also visits to say goodbye to Tim – and showers Peter with early birthday presents – as his fourth birthday is now fast approaching.

It is a shame to say goodbye to someone we have worked with so closely and for so long, but Linda seems keen to get going and the least we can do is try and work co-operatively with her.

Quite honestly, Rob and I feel too excited to dwell on sadness. It will be Peter's birthday in a matter of days – and he has been counting the minutes. The night before his birthday we lay out all his cards and presents across the lounge floor, in preparation for the morning. Friends and family have been enormously generous with their gifts, and we know that Peter will be astonished when he sees what is waiting for him!

He seems a little fazed at first; he is incredulous that all these gifts could be for him. After a few moments, however, a huge smile lights up his face and he starts jumping around the room, squealing and frantically ripping open the wrapping-paper!

He wants to wear his "I'm 4!" badge immediately. Then he wants to blow up all of his balloons, even though his party isn't until the weekend. After a special birthday breakfast, Peter's grandparents arrive, laden with yet more presents, "Dora The Explorer" Lego and a remote control crane! We head off to the seaside, where Peter throws pebbles in the sea. Next, it's to McDonalds for lunch, Peter's choice, naturally, and then the rest of the day is spent having fun on the pier and playing "crazy golf".

Peter's party two days later is a great success and all the children soon head into the garden for a water fight. Mummy somehow gets drenched, which Peter thinks is hilarious! Watching him and his cousins running around screaming and laughing is wonderful.

I simply could not love a biological child any more than I love Peter. All we wish for now is for it to become official. Our thoughts are never far away from the impending court date. We know we have only a few more steps to go before Peter is our legal son. Then nobody will be able to take our little boy away from us. There is always this dark and terrifying thought, preying at the back of our minds.

12

The best laid plans

OCTOBER–NOVEMBER 2004

There are some things in life that fill you with such trepidation that taking the easy option and giving up often seems a better idea. If someone had shown us all the trials and tribulations we'd have to contend with throughout the adoption process, I doubt if either one of us would have felt brave enough to continue.

When you're almost at the end of your journey, however, you somehow learn how to arm yourself against any last, unforeseen obstacles.

Unforeseen obstacles such as a birth mother wishing to reclaim her son – our son Peter – at the very last moment.

Friday 1 October 2004
This is the day when the Guardian *ad litem* comes to our house to meet us for the first time. I am quite resentful that yet another authority figure will be allowed to question our son, and us, for hours at a time. I have it in my head that this man will be a "by the book" sort of chap, who will annoy me greatly.

I am wrong. When the Guardian arrives he is flustered after a disastrous journey lasting many hours. He is so busy lamenting the state of rail travel that any lingering nerves vanish almost immediately. He is an older man, quietly spoken, and with an open manner. Simon, as I shall call him, has met Peter previously at the foster carers' house, when Peter was only two years old. He was the Guardian when the Care Order was made. We assume that Peter will not remember him from so long ago, so we have simply explained that "a friend" is coming for lunch, so as not to worry him unduly.

This, it turns out, is our first mistake, for as we discover, Peter has an astonishing memory. He clearly recalls meeting Simon before, in his bedroom, at the foster carers' house up north. This is extremely unfortunate, as it looks as though Robbie and I have set out to lie to him about who this man actually is. We cannot explain to Peter the job of a "guardian of the court" – but we repeat that he is our friend because he is here to make sure that we stay together as a family – forever.

Simon already seems to know an awful lot about Rob and me. He even knows that I am writing this book, and asks if he will be in it! Peter seems at ease in his company and chats away quite happily, showing Simon all his newly-acquired birthday toys, strewn across the lounge floor. He is proud to introduce our dogs to Simon and particularly keen to tell him what we are having for lunch, food being one of the big loves in his life!

It is only after lunch, while Peter sits watching TV away from the table, that Simon reveals just how much power the Guardian actually has. We had no idea that a Judge will place so much weight on his independent opinion. He explains that his job is to evaluate what is in a child's best interests. Sometimes this involves custody battles, not only adoption cases. He has to present a detailed report to the Judge prior to the court hearing. Simon has met Peter's birth mother and his grandma, and is in no doubt that it is in Peter's best interest for him to stay with us. He seems impressed by how content Peter appears to be; the bond between us is plain to see.

Simon is also bound to record how we feel social services and our adoption agency have acted – whether we've been happy with the way we have been prepared and supported and the way the process has been conducted.

We don't want to gripe unnecessarily, and it is Simon who comments that the delay over the issue of contact with grandma seemed entirely avoidable. Having met grandma himself, he is baffled as to why Clare and her manager thought it appropriate for us to write to this woman. He asks us whether the delay has annoyed us, and obviously we say 'yes', and he says that it would have been far better for everyone concerned, especially Peter, if we had gone to court earlier. It is good to see that Simon feels as we do, that Peter's best interests – and ours as his parents – have sometimes seemed to fall by the wayside.

When Simon looks through the life story books, he is surprised at the amount of detail and the volume of information we have been given. I must admit that I feel the deluge of photos, letters and reports of Peter's history may prove to be somewhat overwhelming for Peter when he is old enough to read it. My friend, who is also adopted, agrees. She thinks that it will be too much for him to take in. I think that the life story books from the last foster carers are too intense: every outing, every mood swing, every smile, and almost every day he spent with them are captured in a photo. How many of us have our "moody moments" caught on film and put in a book? Also, along with these two thick binders came a massive box of everything Peter had ever made, either at nursery or at home. Every drawing, every painted leaf, every home video, was included. When Peter finally moved in with us, four carloads of toys and clothes came too, not forgetting a huge box of trinkets, presents, letters, cards and clothes from his birth mother. So, at times, it really did feel as though our house was being taken over!

Simon agrees that the life story books are very thorough, and is pleased at the amount of effort Peter's social worker has put in. Some social workers have other priorities, apparently. He says his own picture should be included in our current life story book, and we are not sure if he is joking. He is not. We decide to put his photo in the album after the final court hearing, so that Simon will become part of Peter's adoption story.

The rest of Simon's visit goes well. It isn't until the next day that we realise just how upset Peter is at seeing this figure from his past again.

18 October 2004

At home Peter does not display any particular disturbance. This time the nursery is the target of his defiant and aggressive behaviour. They are so worried that they call me in to ask for advice on how to handle him, as he is rejecting their attempts to either pacify or discipline him.

Both Robbie and I try to talk things through with Peter. Almost immediately, he becomes very agitated and tearful, shouting at us that he doesn't like 'that man'. We ask Peter whether he is worried that the man might take him away from us – and the answer is a tremulous 'yes'. We do everything in our power to assure Peter that this man is our friend – a friend who will be making sure he stays with us in our home, forever.

Peter, I remember hugging you so tightly as you bravely smile, wanting to believe us. But soon enough, your nightmares return with a vengeance, along with a new – and very real – fear of the dark. Your behaviour veers from clingy, to angry, to tearful…to quietly reflective. It is similar to your unpredictable behaviour at the beginning of the placement and you begin to ask questions about "court" more and more often, desperately trying to pick up on our telephone conversations and questions from family and friends.

We do our best to protect you, but being such a bright and inquisitive little boy, you want to know exactly what adoption means and why we all have to go to court to see a Judge. Rob and I sometimes have no option but to take telephone calls when you are in the room. You are with us, when we have a call two weeks after Simon's visit – a call telling us that your birth mother is planning to contest the adoption.

Apparently, Peter's birth mother is not only refusing to give her consent, as predicted, but intends actively to oppose the adoption, relying on arguements under the Human Rights Act* to stake a legal claim for Peter to be returned to her care. Rob and I are warned that the final court date may have to be adjourned if she insists on pursuing her claim. This news sends us reeling. One day I end up crying down the phone to Simon. He assures me that, although nothing is ever certain in this world, he will personally "jump off a bridge" if the Judge rules in favour of the birth mother. My head spins and I feel my stomach lurch. I think to myself, 'YOU will jump off a bridge if our son has to be handed back to his mother! What do you think Rob and I will do?'

This is the very woman that Peter has so many nightmares about – not even wanting to look at her photo. To return Peter to her "care" would destroy him. It is such a dark place to go to, that I simply cannot allow myself to think about it. I fear that if I do, I will end up going mad.

Tuesday 19 October 2004
Sure enough, Peter's birth mother arrived at Court in the north of England today, with her solicitor in tow. Clare and Simon were both present and they make immediate contact with us after the hearing.

Clare is clearly livid that Peter's birth mother has the right to have the final hearing adjourned at this eleventh hour. She has never made any effort to amend her ways

---

*The Human Rights Act 1998 incorporated into UK law the European Convention on Human Rights (ECHR). Although the law on dispensing with consent to adoption was not changed, in contested cases more emphasis was, arguably, placed on the 'right to private and family life' under Article 8 of the ECHR.

and, furthermore, when Peter was in foster care, she showed little interest at the pre-arranged contact meetings with him, and never actively tried to regain custody at any point.

I do understand, of course, how hard it must be for her to be asked to free her child for adoption. I also understand that in her own way she loves her son and wants to be given another chance to parent him. Having said that, everyone is aware of her personal circumstances – and that she is in no position to give Peter a loving, secure or safe home. She is sadly deluding herself if she imagines that one day Peter might be returned to her care.

Clare and Simon tell us that the birth mother's barrister will try to explain the facts to her very clearly before the next court hearing, which has been set for 30 November 2004. The final hearing, which we will all have to attend, and which was supposed to be transferred to a family court near to where we live, has been re-scheduled for just before Christmas – in Peter's home town, no less. It appears that if we still want the case to be heard in our local family court, then the proceedings will spill over into 2005 – and this is something we really want to avoid. Having to entertain social workers at our house every few weeks, and the continuing uncertainty are unsettling Peter far too much as it is – we know it has to stop. We would rather drive three hundred miles for a fifteen-minute court hearing (yes – a fifteen-minute hearing and then it's supposed to be all over), than let things drag on into another year.

End October – November 2004

So, as has been the case throughout the adoption process, Robbie and I try to get on with our lives, putting the court dates and the stress to the back of our mind. As my friend says to me around this time, it seems to be an endless round of 'dusting off the armour to commence battle once again', which is a pretty good description of how we are often made to feel. Not just us either, it affects family and friends almost the same. For Peter's sake we try our best to hide any anxiety, and we certainly have a great time celebrating the first year anniversary of Peter moving in to our home.

In some ways Rob and I simply cannot believe that twelve months have passed since we met our son for the very first time. In other ways we simply cannot recall life before Peter. It seems as if he's always been part of the family!

We often speak to Peter about the first time we met him. He vividly remembers waving from the foster carers' front door, watching our big black Jeep as we parked on the driveway. He remembers going to feed bread to the ducks and playing Fuzzy Felt Faces on the floor with us and the foster carers' son.

Peter knows that Clare looked long and hard to find him a special mummy and daddy. We tell him how thrilled and excited we were when we found out WE were going to be his parents. We let him know that it was one of the happiest days of our lives. We explain to him why he had to stay at the foster carers' house until his new mummy and daddy could come and get him. Now, we tell him over and over again, that he will be staying with us forever.

We tell him that although Clare still has to come and visit us – something Peter now hates – she will not be coming for very much longer because soon her "job" will be done. We buy Peter a Cabbage Patch Kid, a boy, called Perry. These particular dolls come with their own adoption papers and birth certificate. It is a great way to talk to Peter about his own adoption order and new birth certificate. Peter seems to understand at least some of what we are saying. He definitely knows that it is all very special. He decides to keep Perry's adoption papers and birth certificate safely under his pillow. He has already decided that HIS new birth certificate will have pride of place on his bedroom wall!

After celebrating our first year together as a family, we wait anxiously to hear whether we are going to have to get a solicitor in order to be legally represented at the dispensation hearing.

With just a couple of weeks to go, we finally receive the best news in the world: Peter's birth mother has changed her mind again and is not going to actively contest the adoption after all! This is fabulous news for us, and although she is still not willing to sign her consent, we will not need a lawyer to represent us. Short of an unpredictable catastrophe, things are looking very good indeed. In fact, when our new social worker, Linda, comes to visit us, she says that it should now be something of a foregone conclusion. We very much hope so, although Clare is not quite as optimistic when we speak on the telephone – not wanting to tempt fate, I suppose.

Monday 29 November 2004

We are only a day away from the dispensation hearing. With more and more talk of court and Clare telephoning regularly, Peter's behaviour has become very unsettled. It changes from extreme clinginess to me, to the most earth-shatteringly loud tantrums – usually in public – where he can have a rather open-mouthed and captive audience!

He asks a huge number of questions, which we try to answer as honestly and gently as we can. He hates me leaving him for even a couple of hours, screaming that I have 'walked away and left' him, and hugging my leg so tight that I fear he will never let go.

He wants his daddy and me to be part of everything he does, down to smelling or tasting his food. He asks us to share his bath, and wants to accompany us everywhere, whether it be to work, the vet, the shops or the toilet. I have to plead with him not to fight with friends' children. He doesn't want to share any of his toys and is reluctant to share mummy too. He is happiest at home with both his parents and the dogs he loves immensely. I think if we could remain in that cocoon indefinitely, then Peter would be the happiest little boy alive.

But it isn't all bad. We have some lovely times too, like at Peter's friend's birthday party at a nearby fun factory. On this particular day Peter is a total joy, winning over all the other parents with his smile and his charm. The tantrum when we leave is pretty award winning, but aside from that, it has been a special time watching him laugh and play with his nursery friends.

Nursery remains an important "constant" in life. Indeed, apart from the last difficult phase, he is now doing remarkably well and we are justifiably proud of him. Consequently, we are distressed when we receive our final court date and realise that Peter is going to miss his Christmas party and Nativity play. Peter's nursery workers immediately understand and arrange to have another Christmas party for Peter on a separate occasion. I am so grateful to them, as I don't want Peter to blame the adoption for missing all the fun.

Tuesday 30 November 2004

So, despite the hitches along the way, our case finally makes it to the dispensation hearing. We know that everything should run smoothly, but Robbie and I still have that familiar uneasy feeling, that knotted ball of tension twisting our stomachs. Our case will be heard at ten in the morning, and should take no more than thirty minutes. Then Clare will ring us with the "expected" good news.

When it gets to midday, and we have still not heard anything, we start to panic.

Finally, just before 12.30, Clare rings to say that everything has gone according to plan. The Judge has dispensed with the birth mother's consent. Clare tells us that Peter's birth mother, although very sad, managed to say that she respects Rob and me as Peter's adoptive parents. I am quietly grateful to her; it means so much and I can only imagine how hard it must have been to say it.

Robbie and I now know that short of some last minute calamity, the final court hearing should be a formality. That night we share a bottle of champagne, as an early celebration. Although still cautious, we are almost sure that nothing else can stand in our way.

As soon as we are Peter's legal parents, the celebrations can really begin!

13

Our dreams come true
DECEMBER 2004

As the final court date draws closer, we hardly dare believe that soon the whole adoption process will be over. It has taken up almost three years of our lives, which is a long time to remain positive and to keep focused on our goal. It has been a tough learning curve: after years of infertility having to prove beyond doubt that we can be committed and loving parents to an adopted child. No matter how hard it has been, we have never given up hope. And the rewards – as almost any adoptive parent will tell you – are enormous. I would go to the ends of the earth for our son.

Sunday 12 December 2004
Every day Rob and I try to explain to Peter what is going to happen and whom we will meet on "Court Day".

He knows that we are going to meet a "judge" – in our case a woman. He knows that Clare, Simon and our new social worker, Linda, will be there too. He also knows that on this special day he will receive an "Adoption Order", with his name on it, and then he will be part of our family forever. Peter already understands that he is our son, and is proud of showing everyone his zip tag with "Special Son" on it. He has been told that the Judge will give him a party bag full of treats when he goes to court. This piece of information seems to make the most impact! That and the fact that he can't wait to wear his new outfit – a brown furry coat and red flashing boots!

We are only a day away from travelling north to our hotel. Having arranged for my parents to look after our dogs, we are soon packed and ready to go. Peter wants us to take the dogs to court, but we have to explain that they probably wouldn't enjoy it! We wonder how Peter is going to feel when he recognises the town where he was born. It could trigger some awful memories for him, and affect his security and behaviour all over again. We are both naturally very concerned about this, though we try not to show it to Peter.

Clare has recommended a hotel away from the main shopping centre, which is where Peter would have spent a lot of time when he was a baby. We are also taking the precaution of arriving after dark, so that Peter will not be too aware of his surroundings.

On the whole, Peter's behaviour is pretty stable – in spite of the fact that Clare insists on coming to our house to say her "official" goodbye today. Rob and I understand why she feels that the meeting is necessary, but we can't quite understand why it has to be right now – when Clare knows that she will see us again in court in two days' time. Furthermore, Linda also insisted on visiting only a couple of weeks ago. This did irritate us, as we feared two visits close together would have an adverse effect on Peter. When I mentioned my concerns to Linda, she calmly reminded me that it was her job, by law, to "home visit" right up until the final court hearing. She is right, of course – though it simply makes us want that final date to be here all the sooner!

Monday 13 December 2004

The journey back to Peter's home town turns out to be psychologically difficult for us all. My stomach screws into the usual tight knot as I wonder how Peter will fare if he starts remembering events from the past. For us, the town brings back memories of our stressful introductions. I am extremely worried that we will run into someone from Peter's birth family. I have visions of our son being snatched – which is plainly ridiculous, I know! I pull myself together for the sake of my family, if nothing else.

We have been advised not to stray too far from our hotel. We decide to stay put and have our evening meal in the hotel restaurant, which pleases Peter. He also enjoys sharing a bedroom with his mummy and daddy – and indeed, wants me to sleep in his bed with him. So, just for once I do, and feel Peter's soft rhythmic breathing close to mine.

Tuesday 14 December 2004
Rob and I hardly sleep a wink and in the morning I am physically sick, due to the stress and excitement. It soon transpires that Peter did recognise landmarks in his home town the previous evening; he asks if we can call in to see the foster carers' son.

It never ceases to amaze us what an incredible memory our son possesses. Apparently it is not unusual for children in care to have vivid flashbacks. Although astounding, it is also heartbreaking, as most of Peter's recollections are not happy, which is precisely why they have left their mark in the first place.

Peter's behaviour remains remarkably even. Robbie and I present him with a specially engraved silver tankard early in the morning, which he uses to have his favourite blackcurrant drink. He is very excited while having his breakfast and cannot wait to get all dressed up to see the Judge. When the taxi arrives to take us to the Court, it is an amazing feeling, knowing that within the hour Peter will legally be our son.

Our hearing is at ten o'clock and we pray that Clare is right when she says that adoption cases are very rarely held up for long. After all, it just would not be fair on the child.

With armed police at the entrance to the courthouse, we are keen to whisk Peter through as quickly as possible. He seems pretty unfazed about the whole thing – even though he is the only child in the building and there are many people hanging around, waiting for their cases to be heard, including two men who have already had a major confrontation outside one of the courtrooms!

We are very glad when Clare appears, laden with presents, I might add, and is soon followed by Linda and Simon. I'm sure my nerves must be apparent to everyone. Almost immediately an usher of the court escorts us to a rather informal dining room – not quite the big, scary courtroom Rob and I have imagined.

By this point Peter's only interest is the contents of Clare's bag of goodies. It is all we can do to stop a tantrum as we desperately encourage him to say 'hello' to the judge first!

The judge is a tall, large, rather forbidding figure, dressed in wig and fine robes, which Peter thinks very amusing. Later he keeps saying she was wearing a funny hat. Rob and I are surprised that the judge is in full attire, as we had been told that this was unlikely for an adoption. It seems a little incongruous in a dining room with china cups and saucers.

Despite initial impressions, the judge is a very pleasant woman and she immediately gives Peter a party bag full of balloons and sweets. Typically, he shoves a brightly coloured lollipop into his mouth straight away – so that for the entire rest of the hearing he can barely utter a word. He does manage to tell the judge about our dogs though, when she enquires after their names.

She jokingly asks ' They don't bite, do they?' and my heart skips a beat. Suddenly I imagine Peter telling an enormous fib and making out that they've mauled and maimed him. Fortunately Peter nonchalantly shakes his head and tells her that they like to lick him a lot, which makes the judge smile. I breathe a sigh of relief and tell myself not to be so jumpy, as nothing is going to go wrong.

The judge then asks Rob and me a few questions about our life with Peter, and she wants to know how he is settling in at nursery. She is also curious about this diary.

Peter has lost all interest by now and is busy opening his colour megasketcher, which is one of the presents from social services. After five more minutes of chat and looking at photos, the judge officially signs the Adoption Order. Then our adoption hearing is over. Clare leans towards us and says, 'He's yours!'

I simply want to cry.

We all stand outside the courthouse in the drizzling rain, having more photos taken for Peter's life story book. Peter still seems preoccupied with his presents. He holds his megasketcher aloft in each and every photo. This particular present has made more of an impact than anything else this day! I can truly say that I haven't felt as happy since my wedding day seven years earlier.

Clare turns to say goodbye, genuine tears in her eyes. Peter poignantly calls after her as she crosses the road and disappears from view. It is the last time that any of us will see her. For all my mixed feelings about Clare, I too feel surprisingly moved at saying a final farewell. Peter gave Clare a china bear and a hand-painted card when she last visited us at home. It explained how we all felt. Clare knows that, no matter what may have been said over the past year, we owe her an enormous amount of gratitude for choosing us to be Peter's parents. We will always be in her debt.

After we say goodbye to Clare and Linda (Rob and I so wish Tim could have been here to share our joy), Simon offers to give us a lift back to our hotel. ' Who knows', he says, as he prepares to bid farewell, 'one day we might all meet again.' This refers to Peter's birth mother and her urgent desire to have another baby. Her personal circumstances have not changed and it is doubtful that she would be allowed to keep a child. Rob and I choose not to reply, apart from smiling and thanking Simon for all his hard work. For the moment, this is something we do not want to think about.

We arrive back at our hotel only an hour after leaving it. Everyone has warned us that the court case might prove to be something of an anti-climax after waiting for so long.

It is not.

It was quick – I will say that. However, I don't think there was any need to draw things out. All the hard work and preparation had been done long before the court hearing – and with a four-year-old trying to grasp what is going on, fifteen minutes is ample. Now all we have to do is wait for the new birth certificate to arrive in the post, which will take approximately six weeks.

We start packing our clothes and get ready to return down south – back to our home, our dogs and our families. Peter is thrilled with all the presents from Clare and her department. They include a silver musical moneybox, a "Spot" video and some fabulous "Adoption Day" chocolate from Thornton's. He is also fascinated by the Adoption Order itself. He recognises his name on it and seems to realise that something very "official" and very important has just taken place. We have not been able to call and see the foster carers' son, so we explain to Peter that he can write a letter as soon as we get home, telling him all about his exciting day in court!

The journey home is long, boring and takes twice as long as we've anticipated. When we finally arrive, Peter runs shouting into the house, excited to be back in his comfort zone again. My parents have left more gifts for us to open, including a beautiful china figure of a boy praying. The boy's face is almost identical to Peter's and I cannot stop gazing at it. It is a wonderful reminder of a momentous day.

All three of us are exhausted, but deeply happy too. It is a quietly reflective moment when we all finally head upstairs to bed that night.

Wednesday 15 December 2004

The next day feels quite odd. Rob returns to work as normal and Peter and I have a quiet time at home, painting, playing, and chatting about the previous days.

Peter hasn't totally grasped that there will be no more "adoption"; how can he, at the tender age of four?

'Not go to court no more Mummy?' he says more than once. 'Court long way away?' he asks a number of times. He keeps on looking at the Adoption Order and announces that he wants it to be hung directly above his bed. We chat about the fact that we will no longer be seeing Clare who has been a constant link for more than two years. He knows that Clare has finished her work with us and any anger he once felt towards her now seems to be replaced by sadness that she is out of his life for good. It is satisfying to realise that Peter has reached a place of contentment and security, where Clare no longer represents either a need or a threat.

In his mind, Peter must have been telling himself a thousand times that this time he would not be moved on again. This time he is staying put. He often talks about "family" and systematically runs through the list of people he loves: mummy, daddy, the dogs, nana and grandad, grandma, uncles, aunts, and cousins. It is very important to Peter to be clear about who his "forever" family is, and he needs to know, and to be told again and again, that they love him very much.

Sunday 19 December 2004

On Sunday after court, we enjoy a family celebration at a nearby restaurant and "fun factory". Peter is being showered with "Adoption Day" gifts and is quite overcome by all the attention he is getting.

His behaviour becomes fairly erratic and he is very hyperactive. He is testing boundaries all over again and is adorable one minute and stubborn and defiant the next. All of this mixed behaviour is entirely expected, of course, and it could be a whole lot worse. Despite a few "stubborn" moments, things run smoothly and Peter and his cousins have a great time. We have taken along the framed Adoption Order to show everyone, and Peter has also brought his silver tankard. Afterwards Peter looks at the photos and remembers what a lovely time he had, and that is the most important thing for us. This handsome little boy is our much longed-for son. And we are a family for keeps.

As we begin the countdown to Christmas, I feel more relaxed than I have done in a long time. This Christmas will feel very different from the last. This Christmas we will enjoy the day like any other family, knowing that our little unit is safe and secure.

What a Christmas that will be!

14

And so to the future

DECEMBER 2004–DECEMBER 2005

This last section of my diary may prove to be as much a record of our learning, as of Peter's progress. It chronicles the past twelve months since Christmas 2004: the good, the not so good, the continuing joy, and the moments of anguish.

It considers the unforeseen problems of mixing with your child's new friends and their parents – difficult if you are hoping to keep your son's adoption private. It also depicts how the best intentioned of acts, something as simple as a cousin's sleepover at our house, can have a quite shocking adverse effect. To reach inside the mind of a mixed up and scared little boy and see the world through his eyes is a humbling experience. When moving from foster home to foster home is the norm, a "sleepover" can be a new and destabilising experience. What we take for granted may be viewed in a wholly different light. Nothing can be expected to be as "normal" for an adopted child – and who defines what is normal anyhow?

The chapter also looks back over the last ten years of our striving to become parents, and particularly at the last three years of this adoption story.

Were we prepared for the home assessment? Did we fully understand the agony of waiting to be "matched" with a child? How close did we come to giving up when things weren't going our way? Did we ever imagine we would be lucky enough to have a son like Peter?

I hope that, above all, this closing chapter – and indeed the whole diary – will prove to anyone considering adoption (or parenthood) that, no matter how hard things may get along the way, there is no greater feeling in the world than being told that a child is yours.

December 2004 – January 2005

So to Christmas again.

Peter is beside himself with excitement and loves telling everyone how Father Christmas is going to come down our chimney and leave a sack full of presents. He insists on leaving out a banana and chocolate cake for Santa and his reindeer. He also leaves some water and blackcurrant juice – and knows Santa has been when the food has gone and the cups are empty in the morning!

Peter is a noticeably different child from the angry and anxious little boy who first moved in with us, some thirteen months ago. It is heart-warming to collect the Christmas cards from his friends on the last day at nursery. They mean so much to Peter, and to us, and he pins them up on the wall as affirmation that he is "liked" by his peers. Spoilt by friends and family alike, one of his favourite presents is a magic set – and he charms his grandparents and cousins with shouts of "Abracadabra" as he pulls a white rabbit out of a top hat!

New Year, as luck would have it, sees Peter erupt with chickenpox. As usual when he is in pain or discomfort, he is almost stoic in his acceptance of the many itchy spots. He doesn't complain much although the outbreak is really quite nasty. But he cannot wait to get back to nursery. Peter absolutely thrives on routine and having to stay at home, not doing very much, is clearly trying his patience!

While he is sick, we receive Peter's new birth certificate, approximately seven weeks after the court hearing in December.

It comes as something of a disappointment as it does not have our names on it after all. It simply states Peter's new name (to which we have added Rob's father's name in the middle), and it gives the date of the adoption. It seems that to obtain the full birth certificate, with our names on it as Peter's parents, we have to send off a cheque for £7, which we do immediately. When the new certificate arrives, Rob and I are not listed under "Mother" or "Father" – but as the adoptive parents. We are happy with that and order another copy for Peter.

So, we can now apply for a passport for Peter and book our first family holiday abroad. And we receive the long-awaited confirmation that Peter has been accepted by the school of our choice.

On a less pleasing note, we get the date of an operation Peter is due to have. We have already deferred the operation twice during the last year, but this time Peter will definitely have to go through with it. The operation is to drain excess fluid from his testicles, a common problem in young boys and one that usually rectifies itself without the need for surgery. Although a relatively simple procedure, we know that such an invasive experience, as well as a general anaesthetic, will have a profoundly unsettling effect on Peter.

So before this rather unpleasant event has to take place, we decide to invite our nephew Luke for a sleepover. Peter loves being with his older cousin and Luke is just as excited at staying with us for the weekend.

February – March 2005
The weekend seems to go well. The boys enjoy lots of boisterous games, as well as quiet times watching "Harry Potter" and playing "football" on the computer.

By the Sunday, however, Peter begins to display some fairly challenging behaviour and the look in his eyes tells us that his mind is working overtime. At a local restaurant he becomes defiant, constantly kicking under the table. He asks more and more anxiously why Luke's mummy hasn't come to stay with us too. 'Karen come and have breakfast with us in the morning?' he asks. 'Why Luke sleeping here Mummy? Where's Luke's mummy gone?'

No matter how many times we tell Peter that Luke is only staying one night and will go home to his family later today, Peter is not reassured. In the end, Rob takes Luke home a little earlier than planned, while I try to explain things to Peter over and over again.

All to no avail, it seems.

For at least the next two weeks Peter repeatedly asks, 'Luke not live here anymore Mummy?' and 'Where's Luke's bed?' as we have folded away the futon. He starts to be more and more challenging as his security is rocked, and he fears he will be "replaced". This is a throwback to a situation at the foster carers' house, when a baby was brought into the family and naturally took up a lot more of the foster carers' time. Peter resents all babies for this reason and he is clearly questioning whether Luke is going to live with us now and take away his mummy and daddy's attention.

He becomes very possessive of our love, though I am led to believe this is entirely normal for an adopted child who has suffered many moves before finally finding a permanent home.

It is another difficult period and nursery becomes something of a minefield – one day Peter is absolutely fine, the next he is launching unprovoked attacks and hurling children to the floor. The nursery is wonderfully supportive, when we explain to them what is troubling Peter, and we begin to realise that the children Peter attacks most are his closest friends that he adores. It appears that he is testing their friendship just as he tests our love. He is also desperately worried about moving again, so night after night we talk to Peter about the adoption and show him the Adoption Order above his bed. We explain that no-one can ever take him away from us and that he is safe and secure at last, something that the majority of children can just take for granted. Slowly we begin to turn another corner. Peter's happiness returns and the angry outbursts diminish dramatically. It has been hard to watch our son suffer.

April 2005

No sooner have we placated and reassured Peter than along comes the dreaded day of the operation.

I have not felt as tense since our court date in December. Although I strive to maintain an air of confidence, I am desperately worried for Peter. Having had numerous operations myself, I can understand worries about being in hospital – especially when you're four years old and acutely aware of change of any sort.

The operation is not in itself serious, and the problem is not yet causing him undue distress. So it is particularly hard to explain why the operation has to be performed in the first place, as it really doesn't appear to be "fixing" anything at all.

On the day of the operation Robbie and I feel the same as any parents watching their child go under a general anaesthetic. If you could change places in that instant, then you would. You look around you on the ward and observe the false cheeriness of all the redundant parents hovering at the bedside, checking their watches every five minutes as they wait for news of their child. You will the time away as your imagination runs riot – every possible disastrous scenario played out in your head until the nurse comes to tell you that everything has gone well.

Unlike us, Peter was in high spirits this morning. Bundling his favourite toys and games into the car, it was almost like we were setting off on holiday. The reality after the operation therefore comes as something of a shock, even though we have tried hard to prepare Peter for weeks in advance. Horribly sick, extremely angry and in considerable discomfort, Peter particularly hates the "tap" inserted in the back of his hand and it is all we can do to stop him wrenching it away. When the doctor administers some anti-sickness drugs and pain relief, we gradually begin to see some improvement. Three hours later and the difference is astonishing.

Peter devours his dinner and chats away happily – so much so that he is allowed home twelve hours after we first arrived at the hospital.

Recuperation and rest for the next three weeks prove to be a little more problematic. Unsurprisingly, Peter's behaviour rockets from mildly grumpy to screaming, biting, and throwing chairs across the room. We are on a rollercoaster again and I get the worst of the angry outbursts, as it was I who took Peter into the operating theatre and I who cuddled him when they put him to sleep. He wants to know why his mummy allowed "them people" to hurt him. It takes many days – weeks, in fact – to persuade him that nobody was trying to hurt him and no one was trying to punish him; that we would take away his discomfort if we could. Goodness knows that we would.

Family and friends do their best to keep Peter happy and occupied, though stopping a little boy from bursting his stitches is extremely hard work! It is a relief when Peter is allowed to go back to nursery.

No longer angry with me, but clingy instead, he tells me how much he misses me at nursery, and constantly kisses me and tells me how much he loves me. It takes a while to regain the balance between needing my unconditional love and understanding that he cannot possess me entirely. I imagine that, after an operation, this sort of behaviour is normal for any young child, and Peter's reaction is magnified tenfold because of the issues from his past.

As Peter's stitches heal so his behaviour also improves

markedly. At nursery he really starts to flourish and is catching up with the other children. Peter had been assessed as "delayed" by at least a year when he first came to us, but he now forges ahead with his letters and numbers and can draw a picture that any child could be proud of. He can write his name and draw his entire family, dogs included. It seems the social workers in our adoption workshops were right when they said that children delayed through neglect in early life will nearly always catch up when placed in a secure, loving and permanent home; with one-to-one attention they can thrive and start to shine.

Peter is also good at sport and can kick a football with impressive accuracy for a child of his age. Whereas before, he had been put with a younger group of children in the nursery, he now sits proudly alongside the other pre-schoolers, including his best friend, Finley. Peter's key worker tells us what a bright child he is – and adorable to boot.

Gradually, Peter begins to realise that he is different from a lot of the other children at nursery (all of them, in fact), because he did not come out of my tummy, he came out of another woman's tummy. We talk about this matter at length. Peter says that he wishes he had come out of my tummy; Rob and I say that we wish it too, but that adoption has made him very special. We tell him about other people who are adopted, so that Peter sees he is not the only one.

Socialising with the parents of Peter's nursery friends is complicated. Rob and I feel that telling about the adoption should really be left to Peter, but this can be difficult when nearly every mum I meet wants to compare notes about childbirth.

We know that it is only a matter of time before Peter will start saying things to his friends, but in the meantime we don't want to tell all and sundry that our son is adopted. This is not because we are embarrassed, and not because we aren't as proud of our son as any other parent. The reason why we do not want to discuss Peter's business with everyone else is because it is precisely that – it is HIS business – and not something for people to gossip about or something to set him apart from his peers.

I can understand families who adopt a child and move to another area. It's one thing for family and friends to know your business but when the saleswoman at Boots comments on the adoption (yes, it happened to me), you begin to realise that news travels fast! I try to stick to my guns, regardless – assuming that when the parents from nursery school find out that Peter is adopted, they will understand our reasons for not broadcasting the news when we first met them.

May 2005

It is spring. Life continues to be good; Peter is making the most of nursery and forming significant friendships with three or four of the children. Soon our gorgeous son will turn five and will be starting school, embarking on yet another chapter in his young, eventful life. It doesn't seem possible. The twenty months since Peter began life as our son have simply sped by. Neither of us could possibly have anticipated the change in our lives, the impact of a wilful three-year-old after nine years of living together with only ourselves and our dogs to worry about.

Nor could we ever have begun to imagine the joy and unbridled fun a child can bring, the hugs, the exuberance, the infectious laughter, and the smile that can win all.

I still look at you Peter and marvel. Your Daddy and I are so immensely proud of what you have achieved – facing so many obstacles and yet finding the courage to learn to love and trust again.

It is now over ten years since Rob and I started out on the journey to parenthood. Realising that there was a problem, we turned to the specialists and entered the punishing arena of infertility; the only couple among our friends unable to have biological children. I look back now and wonder that my girlfriends of that time are still my closest friends today. They were all on the receiving end of my wailing and frustration at some point in the infertility story and their support throughout that time was invaluable.

And then there was a new story: the story of your adoption. A story that began with an idea and led us through training, preparation and assessment to become a reality with the miracle of you.

I still have to pinch myself, Peter, to believe that I am your mummy. I still get a kick out of people commenting on how lovely you are, that you have "my" smile or Rob's green eyes. It is a privilege to have such a brave and loving child to call our own.

June – August 2005

At the start of summer we prepare for our first family holiday abroad. Peter is mostly looking forward to going on an aeroplane – the holiday afterwards takes second place!

Peter loves the airport and the excitement of boarding our flight. We wonder whether the noise at take-off will frighten him and he will want to get off the plane. He is fine, but it comes as a genuine surprise to Peter that there is more holiday to follow – he really thought that the flight was it!

This is where we start to encounter some problems. Peter is horrified that the hire car isn't our Jeep – and yells at Daddy not to get in it, as it 'isn't our car!' Then Peter is put out that the television is in Spanish and sulks because he cannot watch Cbeebies. Overall, he misses the comfort of familiar food at home. As the week goes on, his behaviour becomes more unsettled and we discover how much our trip abroad is disturbing him.

We have some good times too. Peter loves the boats in the harbour at Puerto Banus and the Crocodile Park, where we are allowed to hold a baby crocodile in our arms. He also enjoys the beaches in Marbella – wading into the sea and building sandcastles with daddy.

However, he constantly wants to know when we are going home and his tantrums escalate. Consequently we reschedule our flights and return to England a couple of days early. Peter is very happy with this decision and cannot wait to see our dogs again, and to be in his own bed, surrounded by all his toys.

We arrive back at our house very late at night, though Peter doesn't seem to mind at all. His face is a picture when he sees that nothing has changed while we've been away. His bedroom, his toys, his beanbag, his computer games – everything is where he left it before we went to Spain. He is a different child almost at once, and Rob and I realise that, for the immediate future, holidays in Britain will be the order of the day. The farm holiday last year was a success because we'd been able to maintain routines, and take a lot of "home comforts" with us. This was crucial for Peter's peace of mind and is something we will be particularly aware of the next time we plan a holiday.

Settling into our familiar routine once more, we enjoy the rest of our summer together. Peter has a leaving party at his nursery and we watch him being blissfully happy, playing with all his friends. We enjoy outings with family and friends. We head to the seaside, to nearby farms, we go swimming, ten-pin bowling and to the zoo. We also become owners of a puppy called Pebbles. Our third dog, she becomes very special to Peter, and he sees it as his job to look after her. It gives Peter a sense of responsibility and is further evidence of his caring nature.

So, we come to the end of August. Before we know it, our son's first school day is only one week away; another momentous occasion for Peter and for us.

September – November 2005

I will never forget the first time I see Peter dressed in his school uniform; handsome, he stands to attention like a little soldier, looking so grown up and yet so vulnerable.

Rob and I have been to see the new school and have

taken Peter a number of times now, meeting the teachers and getting Peter used to the surroundings. He is delighted that his two best friends from nursery will be in his class but we suspect that he still doesn't grasp what school is all about. Having discussed the adoption with the school and shared some details of Peter's background, his teacher is aware that everything must be taken at a very slow pace. Any big change to Peter's routine that shakes his security will have a massive impact on his behaviour. School, therefore, will be quite a test.

Two months down the line, it seems we are not wrong. Peter likes playing with his friends, but he is finding the enforced separation from "mummy" very hard, although he is still only going for half days. He is trying to exercise some control over the situation by being extremely aggressive towards his teacher and his classmates. The discipline at school has perplexed him: he cannot grasp why he has to go to this place every day; he misses the more easygoing atmosphere at nursery – and at home.

With hindsight, it seems that nursery has done him no favours in letting him do as he likes. When Peter tries this approach at school, with its more formal aims and set patterns for the day, he comes rather unstuck.

Eventually, in collaboration with the school, we decide that Peter needs play therapy. Absolutely resolute in their support of us as a family, the school helps us to arrange therapy to start after Christmas, when Peter will have completed one full term. They also arrange an assessment by the educational psychologist, who is of the opinion that Peter will settle down given time.

Even though Peter is one of the oldest boys in his class, we decide not to send him full-time to school until after Christmas when he will feel more safe and secure in that environment. There is a lot of flexibility in the first year, and other children in his class are doing the same, so Peter will not feel singled out. The head mistress suggests that I put a lipstick "kiss" on a piece of paper in his pocket every morning as a source of comfort, and this seems to work a treat. Peter is missing his daddy too, so Rob explains that he has to go to work every day and cannot stay at home either. Although somewhat unconvinced by this comparison, Peter at least listens and comes to understand that he is not the only one who has to do things he would rather not!

As Peter's aggression subsides a little, there are fewer incidents of biting and kicking, fewer disturbances in class and less defiance towards anyone in authority. Thankfully for us, there are also fewer parents complaining about our son. This has been particularly hard to handle. Virtually none of the parents know of Peter's circumstances, so they naturally look towards the parents for someone to blame. It has been upsetting, to say the least.

Before the end of term, Peter starts to form some really strong friendships with children in his class. He receives many Christmas cards. The teachers feel that Peter is learning to trust them, he even allows his class teacher to hold his hand on occasions. Academically Peter is coping well. He has caught up with the other children and his teacher, like the nursery staff before her, says what a bright little boy he is. Although we know there is still a long way to go, we are positive that with therapeutic help and caring support Peter will eventually settle down and be extremely happy at school.

And so to Christmas 2005

It is only now, when we have come so far, that I can look back on the adoption process and raise some questions.

Were Rob and I fully prepared for the intrusion of the infamous home study? No, we were not.

But I now understand why a huge amount of investigation is entirely justified. When the welfare of a child is at stake, no one should take any chances. Even if in the back of your own mind you know that you will make good and loving parents, you still must prove it beyond reasonable doubt to a complete set of strangers, who will then decide your fate.

Were we prepared for the fact that my psychiatric treatment during adolescence could have stopped us becoming parents seventeen years later? Absolutely not.

Did we realise that "waiting" was probably one of the hardest things to have to endure? (And Rob and I waited a comparatively short time before being matched with a child. Some adopters can wait for years.) Again, the answer is no.

So, if we knew then what we know now, would we still have chosen adoption?

The answer is yes – most definitely.

But there are some things I would like to see changed.

I would have liked to be more forewarned about how frustrating the process can be. Neither Robbie nor I had any idea just how long everything can take. So a large dose of patience is one of the most vital ingredients for all adopters.

We would have liked more information about the complexities involved in a long-distance adoption such as ours.

We would have appreciated knowing early on that, if you want to adopt a young and reasonably healthy child, you will be in direct competition with many other suitable applicants. And social workers must try to understand how devastating it can be when you are not chosen to be matched with a specific child. It is simply no good saying to people 'do not get emotionally attached to a child', when the prospective adopters have probably been waiting years to become parents. Quite frankly, it is asking the impossible, so a more sympathetic approach on such occasions would be welcome.

The practice regarding "mixed-race" adoptions has to be reviewed, otherwise too many black and "mixed-race" children will remain in care. At any given time there are over a thousand approved adopters in this country waiting to be matched with a child. In this diverse 21st century society, is seems ludicrous to rule out people just because they have a different skin colour. We should ask children themselves what they think.

We would have welcomed more preparation about the purpose of contact with birth families and previous carers. Although we resisted an early meeting with the foster family so soon after he was placed, we now understand how important it is for Peter to have proof that people do not disappear and can still care about him even if he doesn't live with them.

Before I close this diary, I want to list the positive aspects of adoption in 2005 – and there are many.

Nothing can compare to being matched with a child and knowing that they are going to be yours.

Nothing can compare to forming a bond with that child, and watching their confidence, happiness and security grow day-by-day.

Nothing can compare to your child telling you they love you. Nothing can compare to saying it back.

In retrospect I think Rob and I were very lucky with our adoption agency. Tim, in particular, stands out as a great support and a pleasure to work with. Unfortunately they were not all like him. But almost without exception social workers are overworked and stretched to breaking point, so their job is not made easy, and I have the utmost respect for what they do. As Clare revealed, adoption is an emotive issue for social workers too. Clare was the only consistent figure throughout Peter's early life. She saw him at his worst, watched him being moved from pillar to post, and then finally saw him safe and secure with the parents she chose for him. When she said goodbye on that grey, drizzly court day in December, I could only imagine how she must have been feeling.

So that brings me to the end of this adoption diary. Both Rob and I know that the way ahead may not always be straightforward. We are constantly learning from our son and will continue to do so in the future. There will come a time when Peter is old enough to have the letters from his birth mother, and that may prove hard for him to deal with. At least he knows that we write to her once a year to tell her all his news, and that she writes to us. We have made no secret of this. And Peter also knows that we stay in touch with his foster carers – sometimes he likes to write them a card himself, and sometimes he doesn't. There may come a time, in his teenage years, when Peter feels resentful that we are not his "real" parents; he may wish he could have stayed with his birth family.

Despite some misgivings we do not worry unnecessarily about the future, for none of us can know how our children are going to turn out. It is simply our job to love them, guide them, and support them. Without a shadow of a doubt, Rob and I – and our wonderfully close and supportive family – will be behind Peter every step of the way.

I would like you to know, Peter, that not once have we regretted our decision to adopt you – no matter how tough things may have been at times and no matter how much we have felt at odds with the system. Not a day goes by when I'm not thankful to Clare for bringing us together. I sometimes think of your birth mother too, especially now, as we head towards another family Christmas. I thank her for giving you life – she could so easily have chosen a different path. I pray that she may find happiness and contentment, and I promise that we will always look after you, our son, and love you forever.

If anyone reading this is wondering whether adoption might be right for them – I urge you, pick up the phone and start the ball rolling. For if you never do it, you will never know. And just think of what you might be missing...

'Love you to the moon and back,' Peter whispers quietly, as we tuck him into bed at night.

This has been a family tradition for three generations.

'Love you too,' we reply, thinking how very lucky we are to be his parents.